The Economics of Work and Family

Jean Kimmel
and
Emily P. Hoffman
Editors

2002

W.E. Upjohn Institute for Employment Research
Kalamazoo, Michigan

Library of Congress Cataloging-in-Publication Data

The economics of work and family / Jean Kimmel and Emily P. Hoffman, editors.
   p. cm.
Includes bibliographical references and index.
   ISBN 0-88099-246-8 (hardcover : alk. paper)—ISBN 0-88099-245-X (pbk. : alk. paper)
   1. Work and family —United States. I. Kimmel, Jean. II. Hoffman, Emily P.
   HD4904.25.E29 2002
   306.3'6—dc21
                          2002012699

The facts presented in this study and the observations and viewpoints expressed are the sole responsibility of the authors. They do not necessarily represent positions of the W.E. Upjohn Institute for Employment Research.

Cover design by J.R. Underhill.
Index prepared by Diane Worden.
Printed in the United States of America.

The Economics of Work and Family

Dedication

To my amazing kids, David and Elizabeth,
who make my work/family balancing act worthwhile!
J.K.

To my husband, Richard, for all his support.
E.P.H.

Contents

Introduction

Jean Kimmel
Western Michigan University

Each of the six chapters in this volume was first presented as a public lecture as part of the Werner Sichel Lecture-Seminar Series for the academic year 2000–2001. This series is sponsored jointly by the Department of Economics at Western Michigan University and the W.E. Upjohn Institute for Employment Research. The series was titled "The Economics of Work and Family" and included research from six prominent economists specializing in family- and employment-related economic studies. The chapters tackle five broad subjects: child care, parents' time allocation, childbearing decisions, the Family and Medical Leave Act (FMLA), and the relationship between family structure and labor market outcomes.

Each of the authors is a nationally known and widely published expert. However, rather than attempting to present highly technical research evidence, the intent of this volume is to be accessible to readers from a wide variety of backgrounds, including policymakers, social scientists, and college students. In fact, the collection of lectures would serve as a useful companion piece in a course on economics of gender.

Perhaps the most significant problem workers face when attempting to mesh their work lives with their family lives is what to do with young children during parents' work hours. Broadly stated, the child care problems are availability, affordability, and quality. What are the magnitude and scope of these problems, and what might be government's role in alleviating these concerns? The first two chapters in this volume address these topics.

The first chapter, by Professor David M. Blau of the University of North Carolina at Chapel Hill, is titled "Federal Child Care Policy: An Evaluation and Proposal for Reform." Blau, a leader in framing the child care debate in the language and logic of economics, begins by describing the current role of the federal government in subsidizing child care and early education. Next he outlines the sources of market failure in the child care market, and based on this outline he delineates the goals that federal child care policy should address. Finally, centered on these ideal goals, he presents his vision for federal child care policies and illustrates their costs.

As Blau describes, the job of regulating child care falls to the states. At present, the federal government intervenes in the child care market by providing financial support through a number of targeted child care subsidies. After describing the various federal child care subsidy programs, Blau analyzes two broad reasons for federal government involvement in the child care market. First, government intervention might be necessary to help low-income workers achieve self-sufficiency because quality child care is expensive and unaffordable for many lower- or even moderate-income families. Second, the government might play a role in rectifying some of the imperfections in the child care market; for example, parents often do not possess complete information about the overall importance of quality child care nor about the actual quality of care their own children receive. Blau explains that the numerous justifications for intervention can be reduced to two oft-conflicting goals: encouraging parents' employment and enhancing child development.

Blau concludes that the primary goal of child care policy ought to be to strive (within obvious cost constraints) to enhance child development. Using this policy goal, he describes in detail a totally revamped federal child care policy that provides significant child subsidies to parents, who will then be responsible for making their own employment and child care decisions. His proposal offers incentives for purchasing quality care, but they are not contingent on parental employment. Finally, in his conclusion, Blau hopes to influence the child care debate with a clearly devised policy that recognizes trade-offs between different goals and takes a stand behind a single goal— improving child development.

The second chapter, also on the topic of child care, is written by Professor Emerita Barbara R. Bergmann, retired from both American University and the University of Maryland. Bergmann exploits her many years of commitment to the integration of sound economic thought with responsible social policy in her more expansive interpretation of government's role in child care. This chapter, titled "Thinking about Child Care Policy," focuses on the importance of affordable, quality child care to lower-income families and their ability to achieve economic self-sufficiency.

Contrasted with Blau's chapter, Bergmann's piece, while filled with data and computations, is more of an advocacy statement concerning the impact of child care costs on families' standards of living. She summarizes the costs of care and its affordability for families of different income levels. Next, based on these analyses, she develops a workable definition of "affordable" child care and outlines its important characteristics. Finally, she projects the costs of three new child care policy plans, with increasing subsidy eligibility for more families. The plans range from targeting the most disadvantaged families to providing universal coverage. She argues that while these plans are expensive, they are cost-effective and crucial if we as a nation wish to ameliorate the effects of child poverty and encourage self-sufficiency (with an accompanying improvement in quality of life) for disadvantaged families.

Professor Cordelia W. Reimers of Hunter College and the Graduate School of the City University of New York is the author of the third chapter, titled "Parents' Work Time and the Family: Thirty Years of Change." This chapter summarizes the evolution over time in the way that parents divide their time between home activities and paid work. Reimers explains that the enormous changes in work behavior, family incomes, family structure, and fertility rates throughout the last three decades of the twentieth century have worked both to increase and decrease parental time available for their children. This chapter examines the demographic trends in detail and reports the net impact of these trends on parental time devoted to their children.

Reimers details the following five demographic trends: changing family structure (in particular, the rise in single-parent households), increases in parents' combined work time (arising from increased maternal employment and work hours), the surprising stability in median family income, the widening distribution of family income, and declining fertility rates. Reimers uses national survey data for various years spanning the period 1960–1999 from the Current Population Survey, a survey conducted by the U.S. Census Bureau. She includes in her discussion a comparison across race and ethnicity and explains the net outcomes for children arising from these broad trends. She exploits the availability (albeit limited) of data concerning explicit time use by parents. One surprising finding is that mothers' time spent in child care has declined by only 10 percent, with the bigger loss seen in mothers' free time. Additionally, as an increasing number of mothers assume more responsibilities outside the home, fathers have been slow to pick up the slack at home, although their time in unpaid home work has increased somewhat. Finally, Reimers discusses the implications of mothers' market work for their power within the household and the potential consequences of this enhanced power for child well-being.

In her conclusions, Reimers describes several possible policy responses to the rising concerns about the family "time crunch," with a focus on employer responses to the work and family conflict. These include enhanced "flex-time," voluntary shift work, increased possibilities of home-based work, expansion of the Earned Income Tax Credit, and finally, precisely the policies discussed in Chapters 1 and 2 that would affect the affordability and quality of child care.

What are the links between women's childbearing behavior and their employment outcomes? Professor Susan L. Averett of Lafayette College examines this topic in her chapter, titled "Fertility, Public Policy, and Mothers in the Labor Force." Averett focuses first on fertility (childbearing). She explains in nontechnical terms the way that economists model fertility decisions. Then she outlines the relationship between public policy and fertility behavior, with a focus on taxes, welfare policy, Medicaid, and maternity leave. Next Averett turns to a discussion of the employment behavior surrounding childbirth for mothers holding professional jobs, and finally to an examination of the family pay gap: a comparison of the earnings differential between working mothers and women without children who work. In her conclusion, Averett restates the fundamental premise of her chapter: despite having no explicit policies designed to affect fertility rates, it is clear that past and existing policies in the United States *have* had some impact on decision making regarding fertility choice. She concludes that "it is of increasing importance to examine the delicate balance between work and family that many women must maintain," for women all along the income/education spectrum.

Chapter 5, "How Family Structure Affects Labor Market Outcomes," is also related to the topic of fertility and labor force participation. The author, Professor Joyce P. Jacobsen of Wesleyan University, is a prominent researcher of gender issues. Her book, *The Economics of Gender*, now in its second edition, has become a standard reference work in this area. Her chapter summarizes trends in family structure and labor market outcomes, and the reasons the two may and may *not* be related.

Jacobsen begins this discussion by presenting the definition of a family and the meaning of family structure, and the range of labor market outcomes to be examined. Then she presents descriptive evidence about these two concepts and develops the reasoning economists use to explain why there may or may not be a relationship between the two. Finally, she reviews some of the extensive research that has been conducted in this area and considers whether these findings contain any policy relevance. As Jacobsen explains, the mere presence of linkages between family structure and labor market outcomes does not lead necessarily to the conclusion that there is a "problem" for policy initiatives to remedy. The clearest grounds for intervention exist in the realm of labor market outcomes that can be tied to "accidents of birth." That is, none of us is responsible for which family we are born into, and to the extent that birth family circumstance negatively affects future work possibilities, there might be grounds for policy intervention.

Potentially one of the most important policy advances in recent history was the passage of the federal Family and Medical Leave Act (FMLA) in 1993. This landmark legislation mandates 12 weeks of unpaid, job-protected leave each year for eligible workers for care-giving and medical reasons. The FMLA legislation includes as an explicit goal the promotion of economic security for all families. Dr. Katherin Ross Phillips of the Urban Institute has studied this legislation in depth and reports on her findings as well as the broader literature in Chapter 6, "Working for All Families? Family Leave Policies in the United States." She summarizes the existing evidence concerning the utilization of FMLA leaves and analyzes its impact on family economic security.

Phillips begins her discussion by describing the FMLA and explaining its connections to various state and employer leave policies. Then she discusses the importance of access, or eligibility, to this leave coverage, and the linkages between access and family income level. Unfortunately, as is common with other family-related policies, the less that families are likely to have to rely on a federal mandate, the more likely they are to be covered by the FMLA mandate. That is, higher-income families are more likely to have a family member employed in an FMLA-eligible job.

After Phillips discusses access to FMLA leave, she moves on to the discussion of actual take-up of such leave. Because the mandated leave is unpaid, many families simply cannot afford to take it. She describes the types of workers and family members who report having taken such leave and finds that the majority of workers taking FMLA leave report reasons other than childbirth for their leaves. This merely confirms the argument made by the legislation's early proponents that it was truly family policy, not women's policy. Phillips concludes her chapter by describing several policy solutions to the access and take-up problems that she has outlined.

The work/family topics covered in this volume are timely given the passage of family-related legislation such as the FMLA in 1993, as well as the 1996 federal reform of welfare that pushed millions of unskilled single mothers into the workforce. As we as a nation attempt to recover from the current recession and from the lingering economic effects of the September 11, 2001, terrorist attacks, consideration of the factors that facilitate or hinder families' economic security must not be lost.

Finally, I want to use this volume to publicly mourn the untimely death last year of well-known economist and policy researcher Professor Leslie A. Whittington of Georgetown University. She devoted her academic career to studies intended to enhance our understanding of the linkages and conflict between work and family. She, along with her husband and two young daughters, was killed in the September 11 terrorist attacks. Any dialogue and informed policy debate that stems from this volume would be a fitting memorial to Professor Whittington.

1

Federal Child Care Policy
An Evaluation and Proposal
for Reform

David M. Blau
University of North Carolina, Chapel Hill

INTRODUCTION

Child care in the United States is a problem. This is the message of
many newspaper and magazine articles, conferences, and reports by
think tanks and government agencies. Depending on whom you ask,
the child care problem endangers the well-being of children, causes
financial hardship and stress for families, makes it nearly impossible
for low-income families to work their way off welfare, causes substantial productivity losses to employers, and prevents many mothers from
maintaining productive careers in the labor force. The federal government plays a major role in the U.S. child care market, providing subsidies worth almost $20 billion.[1] Are these subsidies well spent? Do they
help accomplish the goals of federal child care policy? What are the
goals of federal child care policy, and how do these goals relate to the
nature of the child care problem in the United States? This chapter
addresses these questions from an economics perspective. The goal of
the chapter is to reach some conclusions about whether child care policy is sensible, and if not, how it could be improved.

An economics perspective on this issue is helpful because it
focuses attention on the rationale for government intervention in the
child care market. The two main arguments that have been made in
support of government intervention in child care are based on attaining
economic self-sufficiency and correcting child care market imperfections that result from imperfect information and externalities. If we
believe that the child care market is inefficient as a result of some kind

of market failure, we can then examine whether government policy is directed appropriately at the cause of the market failure. The key is to identify the source of the market failure. Child care costs as a barrier to economic independence for low-income people suggests a different approach to child care policy than market failure related to the quality of child care. The crucial issue in evaluating whether child care policy is sensible is determining which, if either, of these problems are important in practice in the child care market. This chapter discusses and evaluates the evidence on child care costs as a barrier to economic independence and the evidence on market failure in child care.

The second section of the chapter describes the main features of current federal child care subsidy policy. The next section then discusses in more detail the possible sources of market failure and evaluates the available evidence on them. In the fourth section, I propose a set of principles that I believe should guide child care policy. These principles are based in part on the evidence regarding the importance of alternative sources of child care market failure, but they are also based on my own views about what the goals of child care policy should be. This is inevitably subjective, and I try to be clear about the views I have on the topic. The fifth section evaluates existing child care policy in light of the guiding principles and finds that there is much room for improvement. Next I propose a new set of child care policies that are more consistent with the principles that I believe should guide child care policy. I discuss the rationale for the new proposal and present some illustrative calculations of its cost. The final section contains a summary and conclusions.

U.S. CHILD CARE SUBSIDY POLICY

Child care subsidies help parents pay their expenses for nonparental child care and preschool, and help child care providers pay the cost of providing such care. Some of the subsidy programs are restricted to employment-related child care expenses, while others have no employment requirement. The goals and structure of employment-related child care subsidy programs are quite different from those of early education preschool programs. Society faces a trade-off in child care policy between the goals of improving child well-being and increasing the net return from employment for parents of young children. Thus it is important to interpret child care subsidies broadly and include in the discussion all programs that help defray expenses for the regular care of young children by adults other than their parents. A subsidy for work-related child care expenses may affect the quality of child care purchased, whether or not this is a goal of the subsidy program, and a subsidy for an early education program intended to improve child development affects the work incentives of the parents, whether by design or not.

The goals and main provisions of the major U.S. child care and early education subsidy programs are summarized in Table 1.[2] The first two programs listed are tax subsidies. The exclusion from taxable income of employer-provided dependent care expenses (EEPDCE) is a fringe benefit offered by some firms to their employees in one of two forms. First, if the firm provides child care benefits to its employees in the form of subsidized on-site or near-site facilities or direct reimbursement of employee expenses, such benefits are treated as a form of non-taxable compensation, such as health insurance. Only 4 percent of employees in private establishments had such benefits in 1995–1996 (U.S. Department of Labor 1998). Second, if the firm provides its employees with the option of a flexible spending or reimbursement account ("cafeteria plan") that can be used for child care expenses, the employee contribution to such an account is treated as nontaxable compensation. Twenty percent of private sector workers in 1995–1996 worked for a company that had established a reimbursement account to cover child care expenses.

The Dependent Care Tax Credit (DCTC) allows taxpayers with an adjusted gross income (AGI) of less than $10,000 to receive a tax credit of 30 percent for child care expenses of up to $4,800 per year for two or more children ($2,400 for one child). The subsidy rate declines by one percentage point for each $2,000 increase in AGI, reaching 20 percent for AGI of $28,000. The subsidy rate remains constant for an AGI above $28,000. This subsidy is *means-tested* in the sense that the value of the subsidy declines as income increases. More importantly, however, the credit is not *refundable*, so the amount of credit available to low-income families is relatively small. A nonrefundable credit is limited to the amount of income tax liability; many low-income fami-

Table 1 Summary of the History, Goals, and Provisions of Major Federal Child Care and Early Education Programs

Program	Dependent Care Tax Credit	Exclusion for Employer-Provided Dependent Care Expenses	Title XX Social Services Block Grant	Child Care and Development Fund	Head Start	Child and Adult Care Food Program[b]	Title I, Part A of the Elementary and Secondary Education Act
Acronym	DCTC	EEPDCE	TXX-CC	CCDF	HS	CCFP	Title I-A
Year began	1954	1981	1975[a]	1996	1965	1968	1965
Goal	Subsidize employment-related dependent care expenses.	Subsidize employment-related dependent care expenses.	Help low-income families achieve self-sufficiency; prevent child neglect.	Help families who recently left welfare for work maintain self-sufficiency. Help families who need child care in order to work and are at-risk of going on welfare if child care is not provided.	Improve the social competence, learning skills, health, and nutrition of low-income children aged 3–5.	Improve nutrition of low-income children. Part of the National School Lunch Act.	Provide programs and services for educationally disadvantaged children (children who are failing or at risk of failing student performance standards).

	Nonrefundable tax credit	Employer assistance	Social services block grant	CCDF / TANF	Part-day preschool	Cash subsidies	Grants to states
Form	Nonrefundable tax credit.	Amounts paid or incurred by an employer for dependent care assistance provided to an employee are excluded from the employee's gross taxable earnings.	Block grant to states that can be used for many social services; 15% on average used for child care.	Block grant to states. States must meet maintenance of effort and matching requirements for some of the funds. States may transfer up to 30% of their TANF block grant funds into the CCDF. States may also use TANF funds directly for child care, without transferring them to CCDF.	Part-day preschool, health screening, nutrition and social services.	Cash subsidies for meals and snacks in day care centers and family day care homes.	Grants to states based on number of children from low income families and per-pupil education expenditures.
Provisions	30% tax credit on expenses up to $4,800 for 2 children for AGI$\leq$10K; subsidy rate falls to 20% for AGI>28K.[c]	Up to $5,000 per year excludable. Expenses excluded from gross income are not eligible for the DCTC.	Child care must meet state regulatory and licensing standards.	Sliding fee scale, but states may waive fees for families below the poverty line. At least 4% of the funds must be spent on quality-improvement and consumer education. Child care must meet state licensing and regulatory standards. Contracts or vouchers. Relative care eligible if provider lives in a separate residence.	Free	Child care must meet state regulatory standards. Must serve mainly low-income children.	A school or local education agency may operate a preschool program.

(continued)

12

Table 1 (continued)

Program	Dependent Care Tax Credit	Exclusion for Employer-Provided Dependent Care Expenses	Title XX Social Services Block Grant	Child Care and Development Fund	Head Start	Child and Adult Care Food Program[b]	Title I, Part A of the Elementary and Secondary Education Act
Acronym	DCTC	EEPDCE	TXX-CC	CCDF	HS	CCFP	Title I-A
Year began	1954	1981	1975[a]	1996	1965	1968	1965
Eligibility criteria	Both parents (or only parent) employed.	None	States choose income eligibility. Employment required.	Family income no more than 85% of state median income, but states can (and most do) impose a lower income eligibility limit. Children under age 13. Parents must be in work-related activities.	Kids 0–5 (mainly 3–5); 90% of enrollees must be below the poverty line. 10% of slots reserved for disabled children.	Subsidy amount depends on whether income of children from <130% of poverty line; 130–185% of poverty line; or >185% of poverty line.	Target funds to schools with the highest percentage of children from low-income families.

[a] Earlier provisions of the Social Security Act provided federal matching funds to the states for social services.

[b] Less than 2% of the funds in the food program go to adult care centers.

[c] Beginning in 2003, the maximum credit rate will be 35% for AGI ≤ 15K and the limit on expenses will be $3,000 for one child and $6,000 for two or more children.

SOURCE: Committee on Ways and Means (1998) and U.S. Department of Education (1996).

lies have no federal income tax liability and therefore cannot receive any tax credit. Data from the Internal Revenue Service indicate that 27.4 percent of the total amount of tax credit claimed in 1999 went to families with an AGI of less than $30,000, but almost all of this amount was claimed by families with an AGI between $15,000 and $30,000; only 0.8 percent of the total was claimed by families with an AGI less than $15,000 (Internal Revenue Service 2001, Table 3.3).

In 1996 the Personal Responsibility and Work Opportunity Reconciliation Act (PRWORA) consolidated four existing employment-related child care subsidy programs for low-income families into a single child care block grant program called the Child Care and Development Fund (CCDF).[3] The main goal of the consolidated program is to facilitate the transition of families from welfare to work and to help low-income parents maintain employment. States can use CCDF funds to assist families with income up to 85 percent of state median income (SMI) but are free to use a lower income-eligibility criterion. Parents must be employed, in training, or in school, although some exceptions are permitted. In general, priority for CCDF funds is supposed to be given to families with very low incomes and with children who have special needs. The CCDF also requires that part of the funds be used to assist working poor families who are not currently, recently, or likely future welfare recipients. As part of the general increase in flexibility provided by PRWORA, states are permitted to transfer up to 30 percent of their Temporary Assistance for Needy Families (TANF)[4] block grant funds to the CCDF to be used for child care, and states can also use TANF funds directly for child care services without transferring the funds to CCDF. States must offer "certificates" (formerly called vouchers) that allow families to purchase care from any provider that meets state regulations and licensing standards or is legally exempt from licensing, including relatives and baby-sitters.

The states have substantial flexibility in designing their CCDF programs, including the income eligibility limit, co-payments by families, and reimbursement rates to providers. Only nine states set income eligibility at the maximum allowed by law, 85 percent of SMI. Seven states set the income eligibility limit at less than 50 percent of SMI. States are permitted to waive fees (co-payments) for families with income below the poverty line, and there is substantial variation among states in use of this provision. Fees are determined in many different

ways, including flat rates, percent of cost, percent of income, and com-
binations of these. States are required to have sliding scale fee structures, with fees that rise with family income. The amount of the
subsidy is supposed to be based on a recent market survey, with the
subsidy set to cover the fee charged by the provider at the 75th percentile of the market rate distribution. In practice, many states use out-of-
date market surveys or set the subsidy below the 75th percentile
(Adams, Schulman, and Ebb 1998, p. 23).

The other main means-tested subsidy program with an employment focus is the Title XX Social Services Block Grant (TXX). This
program subsidizes a wide variety of social services and gives states
flexibility in how the funds are allocated across the various eligible services. On average, about 15 percent of TXX funds have been spent on
child care in recent years. Child care funded by Title XX must meet
applicable state standards, and it is often provided through "slots" in
centers and family day care homes purchased through grants and contracts with state or local agencies. States choose the income eligibility
limit.

The last three programs listed in Table 1, Head Start, the Child
Care and Adult Food Program (CCFP), and Title I-A of the Elementary
and Secondary Schools Act, are intended to improve child well-being,
and these programs therefore have no employment or training requirement for the parents. Head Start provides part-day preschool, along
with health, nutrition, and social services, to children from families in
poverty. The goal of the program is to improve the social competence,
learning skills, health, and nutrition of children. Head Start programs
must meet a set of federal standards that are more stringent and child-
development-oriented than most state regulations. The CCFP provides
subsidies for meals meeting federal nutrition requirements served in
licensed day care centers and family day care homes serving low-
income children. Subsidy rates depend on family income of the children served, with a maximum income of 185 percent of the poverty
level. The goal of Title I-A is to provide services for educationally disadvantaged children who are at risk of failing to meet student performance standards. Most Title I-A funds go to schools serving K-12
students, but state and local education agencies may use such funds to
serve preschool aged children as well, in school-based or community-

based programs. Title I-A programs must meet the Head Start standards.

Table 2 summarizes federal and state expenditures on child care subsidies in recent years, and the numbers of children served by the subsidy programs. Assuming that fiscal year (FY) 1999 CCFP expenditures are the same as in FY1997 (in real terms), and that FY1999 real CCDF expenditures are the same as in FY1998, a rough figure for total federal and state expenditure on child care subsidies in FY1999 is $18 billion. A meaningful total for the number of children cannot be computed. Head Start and the CCDF are the two biggest programs in terms of expenditures, at $5.5 billion each. Head Start is the best-funded program per child served, with annual expenditures of $5,759 per child versus $3,400 per child in the CCDF. The only subsidy programs that are open-ended entitlements are the EEPDCE and DCTC tax subsidies (in terms of number of children served, not expenditures per child). The other programs are capped entitlements, with no obligation to serve all eligible families. It is estimated that the CCDF serves only 15 percent of eligible children (Administration for Children and Families 1999). Head Start is estimated to serve 34 percent of 3- to 5-year-old children in poverty.[5] No figures are available on the percentage of eligible children served for the other programs.

WHY SUBSIDIZE CHILD CARE?

The two main arguments that have been used in support of government subsidies to child care are based on attaining economic self-sufficiency and correcting child care market imperfections.[6]

Self-Sufficiency

Child care subsidies might help low-income families be economically self-sufficient, which in this context means employed and not enrolled in cash-assistance welfare programs. Self-sufficiency might be considered desirable because it may increase future self-sufficiency by inculcating a work ethic and generating human capital through on-the-job training and experience, and it may therefore save the govern-

Table 2 Federal and State Expenditures and Children Served by Major Federal Child Care Subsidy Programs

	DCTC[a]	EEPDCE[b]	HS[c]	TXX-CC	CCFP	CCDF	Title I-A[o]
Federal and state expenditures (billions of constant 1999 dollars)							
2000	2.200	0.984	5.056	0.222[d]	1.624[g]	—	—
1999	—	0.995	4.658	0.285[e]	—	9.132[j]	2.015
1998	2.649	0.910	4.443	—	—	6.540[j]	—
1997	2.464	0.862	4.132	0.384[f]	1.582[h]	4.535[j]	—
1996	2.663	0.823	4.223	0.374[f]	1.678[h]	—	—
1995	2.518	0.792	3.862	0.453[f]	1.603[h]	3.4[k]	—
Children served (millions)							
2000	—	—	0.858	—	—	—	
1999	—	—	0.826	—	—	1.760[l]	
1998	6.120	—	0.822	—	2.6[i]	1.531[l]	
1997	5.796	—	0.794	—	2.2[l]	1.248[m]	
1996	6.003	—	0.752	—	2.4[l]	—	
1995	5.964	—	0.751	—	2.3[l]	1.445[n]	

NOTE: See Table 1 for definitions of the program acronyms. Current dollar expenditures were converted to constant 1999 dollars using consumer price index values of 1.093, 1.062, 1.038, and 1.022, 1.0, and 0.96 for 1995 through 2000, respectively. Blank cells indicate that data are not available. This table is from Blau 2001a, Table 8.2.
[a] Committee on Ways and Means 2000, 816. The figure for 2000 is estimated (600). The 1998 figures are preliminary. Figures in the lower panel are number of returns filed claiming the credit, not the number of children. The figures are for calendar years, not fiscal years.

b Office of Management and Budget 1996, Table 5-1. These figures are for the calendar year. The method used to compute them is unclear, and in budget statements for subsequent years they are different. They are also different in Joint Committee on Taxation (1999). These are probably the least reliable figures in the table.

c Head Start Fact Sheet 2001.

d Thirteen percent of $1.775 billion, multiplied by 0.96 to convert to 1999 dollars (Committee on Ways and Means 2000, 600).

e Estimated at 15 percent of $1.9 billion for TXX from Committee on Ways and Means (2000, 634).

f Committee on Ways and Means 1998, 714, 720: 14.8 percent of total TXX funding of $2,800 billion, $2.381 billion, and $2,500 billion for fiscal years 1995, 1996, and 1997.

g Committee on Ways and Means 2000, 600.

h Committee on Ways and Means 1998, 679, 687.

i U.S. Department of Agriculture 2001.

j I computed these figures by summing all federal and state expenditures on the CCDF, either directly or through transfers to TANF, using data from the annual TANF reports to Congress (U.S. Department of Health and Human Services, various years) and reports from the Child Care Bureau (various years). The latter source provides allocations to the CCDF for fiscal years 200 and 2001, but there are not data available on transfers from TANF for these years. Transfers to TANF constituted about half of CCDF spending in fiscal year 1999.

k U.S. General Accounting Office 1998, 4; total funding for the four programs later consolidated into the CCDF: AFDC-CC, TCC, ARCC, CCDBG.

l Administration for Children and Families 2000a.

m Administration for Children and Families 1998, 1.

n Sum of AFDC-CC, TCC, ARCC, and CCDBG Administration for Children and Families 1995.

o U.S. General Accounting Office 1999, 6: Department of Education programs: Title I-A, Individuals with Disabilities Education Act, Even Start, Twenty-First Century Learning Centers. U.S. General Accounting Office (2000b) gives different figures, and an estimate of 341,000 preschool children served by Title I-A and Even Start.

ment money in the long run (Robins 1991, p. 15). These arguments explain why many child care subsidies are conditioned on employment or other work-related activities such as education and training. Child care and other subsidies paid to employed low-income parents may cost the government more today than would cash assistance through TANF. But if the dynamic links suggested above are important, then these employment-related subsidies could result in increased future wages and hours worked and lower lifetime subsidies than the alternative of cash assistance both today and in the future. Note that this argument has nothing to do with the effects of child care on children, and there are few restrictions on the type and quality of child care that can be purchased with employment-related subsidies such as the CCDF and DCTC.

There is surprisingly little known about wage growth of low-skilled workers, but a recent paper by Gladden and Taber (2000) provides some useful evidence. Using panel data from the National Longitudinal Survey of Youth, they analyze wage growth of individuals with no more than a high school education over the first ten years after completing schooling. They find that wage growth rates as a function of labor market experience are very similar for different skill groups, as defined by education (high school graduate or high school dropout). The fact that the lower-skilled groups have wage growth rates similar to the higher-skilled groups suggests that low-skilled workers do gain higher wages by being employed. But the actual wage growth rates with experience are modest for all skill groups, and do not seem high enough to lift low-skilled workers out of poverty. For example, high school dropouts averaged 4.4 percent wage growth per year of actual work experience over the first 10 years of work. Thus, if a high school dropout began working at the minimum wage of $5.15, after 10 years of work experience her wage rate would have increased to $8.00. This is not negligible but is also not enough to significantly reduce dependence on welfare. Gladden and Taber conclude from their results that ". . . low-skilled workers will not have huge wage gains from work experience" (p. 189).

Middle- and upper-income families are generally not at risk of going on welfare, so why should the government provide subsidies for the employment-related child care expenses of such families through the DCTC and EEPDCE tax programs? There is no apparent economic rationale for such subsidies. They appear to be purely a redistribution of the federal tax burden from taxpayers who use paid child care to those who do not, in much the same way that the mortgage interest deduction redistributes the tax burden away from homeowners and toward nonhomeowners. In the absence of any economic rationale for middle-class child care subsidies, the most likely explanation for the existence of such subsidies is that they are politically popular.

Market Imperfections

The other main argument in favor of government child care subsidies is the existence of imperfections in the child care market. The imperfections that are often cited are imperfect information available to parents about the quality of child care, and positive external benefits to society generated by high-quality child care. Walker (1991) spells out these points in detail; the discussion here follows his arguments closely (see also Council of Economic Advisers 1997; Magenheim 1995; and Robins 1991). Imperfect information in the child care market exists because consumers are not perfectly informed about the identity of all potential suppliers, and because the quality of care offered by any particular supplier is not fully known. A potential remedy for the first problem is government subsidies to Resource and Referral (R&R) agencies to maintain comprehensive and accurate lists of suppliers. This may not solve the problem in practice because of very high turnover and unwillingness to reveal their identity among informal child care providers. The second information problem is caused by the fact that consumers know less about product quality than does the provider, and monitoring the provider is costly to the consumer. This can lead to moral hazard (hidden action) and/or adverse selection. Moral hazard is a plausible outcome in day care centers (for example, changing diapers just before pick-up time). Adverse selection of providers is plausible in the more informal family day care sector: family day care is a very low-wage occupation, so women with high wage offers in other occupations are less likely to choose to be care providers. If the outside wage offer is positively correlated with the quality of care provided, then women who choose day care would offer lower-quality care than would the potential caregivers who choose other occupations.

Is there evidence that child care consumers are not well informed? Walker (1991) reports that 60–80 percent of child care arrangements made by low-income parents are located through referrals from friends and relatives or from direct acquaintance with the provider. This suggests that consumers may not be well informed about a wide range of potential providers, but it does not prove that a suboptimal amount of information is used by consumers. Using data from the "Cost, Quality, and Outcomes" study Helburn (1995) and Cryer and Burchinal (1995) report a direct comparison of parent ratings of various aspects of their child's day care center classroom with trained observer ratings of the same aspects. The results show that parents give higher average ratings on every item than do trained observers, by about one standard deviation on average for preschool age classrooms and by about two standard deviations on average for infant/toddler rooms. The instrument containing these items, The Early Childhood Environment Rating Scale (Harms and Clifford 1980), is of demonstrated reliability when administered by trained observers, so this suggests that parents are not well informed about the quality of their child care arrangements. Sonenstein (1991) reports that low-income mothers express greater satisfaction with their child care arrangements when they believe it is convenient, reliable, and low cost than when they believe it is high quality.

The evidence suggests that there may be an information problem in the child care market, but it does not rule out other possibilities. For example, parents could be aware of the developmental benefits of high-quality child care but place low value on those benefits compared with other things they can buy. Parents might feel that their own influence on the development of their children can make up for the effects of low-quality child care, or that the developmental outcomes measured by standard assessments are less important than, say, religious values, respect for authority, and other intangible attributes of child care.

Child care subsidies targeted at high-quality providers could induce parents to use higher-quality care by reducing the relative price of such care. This would not necessarily remedy the information problem, but it would deal with a consequence of that problem, namely a level of child care quality that is suboptimal from the perspective of society. Head Start and Title I tend to provide subsidies for high-quality child care for low-income children, while other subsidies generally place few restrictions on quality.[7]

The externality argument is a standard one that closely parallels the reasoning applied to education. High-quality child care leads to improved intellectual and social development, which in turn increases school-readiness and completion. This reduces the cost to society of problems associated with low education: crime, drugs, teenage pregnancies, and so forth. If parents are not fully aware of these benefits, or if they account for only the private rather than the social benefits of high-quality child care, then they may choose child care with less than socially optimal quality. This argument could rationalize subsidies targeted to high-quality providers, such as Head Start, and could rationalize similar programs for middle- and upper-income children.

Evidence on the effect of child care quality on child development is of two main types. The first is from randomized assignment studies that have evaluated the impact of high-quality preschool programs for disadvantaged children. A comprehensive review of early childhood interventions by Karoly et al. (1998) concludes that such programs can provide significant benefits to participating children and can reduce future expenditures on welfare, criminal justice, and related items. This evidence is compelling, but it is based mainly on very intensive and costly programs that are of higher quality than even Head Start. It is unclear whether child care of moderately high quality provides positive but proportionately smaller developmental benefits, or whether there exists a threshold of quality below which benefits are negligible. The second type of evidence is from observational studies of children placed by their parents in child care arrangements of varying quality. Such studies have generally not followed the children long enough to determine whether any observed developmental gains are long-lasting and whether there are subsequent effects on school outcomes. Hence, there is very little evidence about externalities in the child care market.

WHAT PRINCIPLES SHOULD GUIDE CHILD CARE POLICY?

The following principles are based both on my reading of the evidence and on the goals that I believe a child care policy should attempt to achieve. The latter are obviously based on my opinion.

Child care policy should be neutral with respect to employment. There are no compelling economic or moral reasons for society to encourage employment of both parents in a two-parent middle-class family. Although many parents may feel that two incomes are necessary for a reasonable standard of living, there is no reason why society should provide them with a subsidy to defray the child care costs associated with achieving the desired standard of living. There is a more compelling case for society to encourage single parents to achieve economic independence through employment, but a child care subsidy is at best an indirect and at worst an ineffective approach to accomplishing this goal. A wage subsidy such as the Earned Income Tax Credit (EITC) or a job skills training program are more direct approaches to dealing with the underlying source of welfare dependence, low skills and the resulting low wages. Instead of subsidizing employment of parents, government should, if anything, subsidize the costs of raising children, without favoring market child care costs over the foregone earnings cost of a parent who stays home to care for a child.

Child care policy should provide information to parents about the benefits of high-quality child care and about how to discern the quality of care. In my view, quality is the crux of the child care problem. If parents lack information about the benefits of high-quality child care or do not know how to recognize it, then children suffer as a result. The evidence on these points is not overwhelming, but it is persuasive enough that I would prefer the government take action rather than risk harm to children. If effective and low-cost policies to provide information can be designed, then this would be a good approach because it directly addresses the source of the inefficiency.

Child care policy should provide incentives for parents to choose high-quality care. These policies would be worthwhile, because as noted above some parents who are fully informed about the benefits of high-quality child care may nevertheless fail to choose it. Financial incentives can be a potential remedy for this problem.

Child care policy should give providers an incentive to offer high-quality care. If consumers are given incentives to choose high-quality child care, providers will have an incentive to offer such care. This is the essential feature of a competitive market: firms can prosper only by offering the services for which consumers are willing to pay. Nevertheless, it is possible that the child care market may not be able to respond to a large increase in the demand for high-quality care without a substantial increase in the price of such care. Many high-quality day care centers and preschools are nonprofit establishments that rely on donated space and volunteer labor. They may be unable to expand their capacity enough to absorb large numbers of additional children. For-profit providers will have an incentive to increase quality in response to consumer demand, but they may lack the knowledge and resources to upgrade quality rapidly. Hence, a government policy to help defray the cost of improving quality may be worthwhile.

Child care policy should be progressive: benefits should be larger for children in low-income families. Children in low-income families are at greater risk of developmental delays and the problems that result from such delays. It makes sense that the benefits of high-quality child care are thus larger for these children, and there is some evidence to support this presumption (Currie 2001). Equity considerations also favor a progressive child care policy. This is, of course, purely a personal judgment, not a logical consequence of economic analysis, but it is a compelling judgment to me.

Child care policy should be based on incentives, not regulations. Regulating an industry with a few large firms, such as long-distance telecommunications, is difficult enough. Regulating an industry such as child care with hundreds of thousands of providers is likely to be either very costly or ineffective. Given the relatively small enforcement budgets of most states (U.S. General Accounting Office 2000a), it is not surprising that state child care regulations appear to have relatively little impact on the child care market (Blau 2001a, Chapter 8). I would not discourage the states from regulation, but I would not base federal child care policy on regulation. Financial incentives are more flexible than regulations and if designed well can be self-enforcing rather than requiring a monitoring bureaucracy.

Child care policy should be based on the presumption that well-informed parents will make good choices about the care of their children. Government can provide the best available information to influence parental decision making, and it can provide incentives to make good choices for children. But government should not limit the freedom of parents to arrange care for their children as they see fit, subject to caveats about neglect and abuse. Not all parents will want to take advantage of subsidized high-quality child care in preschools and family day care homes. Some will prefer care by a relative or close friend, some will prefer care in a church-based setting that emphasizes religion, and some will prefer a baby-sitter in the child's home. These choices may not be optimal from a child development perspective, but society should not be in the business of coercing parents to raise children in a particular way. As long as safety and general well-being are assured, parents should be the decision makers. Government policy should inform parents of the benefits of high-quality child care and encourage its use, but it should not require it.

WHAT ARE THE PROBLEMS WITH CURRENT CHILD CARE POLICY?

The majority of child care subsidy dollars are independent of the quality of care under current child care policy. Most of the child care subsidies provided under the CCDF are in the form of certificates (vouchers) that can be used for any legal child care arrangement. The DCTC and the EEPDCE are also unrestricted subsidies that are not tied to the quality of care. The CCFP does not impose any quality standards beyond existing state regulations. Head Start and Title I-A are the only major subsidy programs that require high quality. The latter two programs account for only 43 percent of all child care subsidies according to the information in Table 2.

The reason for this is clear: most child care subsidies are intended to defray work-related child care expenses. In fact, Head Start and

Title I-A are typically not even thought of as child care subsidies, but rather as early education programs for disadvantaged children. They are not designed to facilitate parental employment and are therefore generally not classified as child care programs. But setting aside labels, employment-related and child development–related programs share two common features: they subsidize care of a child by someone other than the parent, which reduces the cost to the parent of being employed, whether by design or not. And they affect child development through the quality of the care provided, again whether or not this was intended. Because they have the explicit goal of facilitating employment, "child care" subsidies emphasize care that is convenient for employment, i.e., full-day care, and are neutral with respect to quality. "Early education" programs emphasize quality rather than facilitating employment, and as a result are often part-day. Conceptually they are the same kinds of programs, located at different points on the two-dimensional continuum of quality and employment facilitation. Viewed in this way, the problem with federal child care policy is clear, at least to me: more than half of subsidy dollars require employment but not quality.

The goal of employment-related child care subsidies targeted at low-income families is to help families achieve and maintain economic self-sufficiency as an alternative to dependence on welfare. If child care subsidies make employment more attractive, and if skills improve through on-the-job training and experience gained by being employed, then child care subsidies would indirectly address the problem of low skills, which is the source of the welfare dependency problem. In this case, child care subsidies would help families escape poverty and welfare dependence in the long run. But as noted above, the typical low-wage job does not provide fast enough wage growth to lift the worker out of poverty. In this case, the child care subsidy must be continued indefinitely in order to make employment attractive, and the goal of economic independence is not achieved. One form of dependence on government assistance, a cash benefit, is simply replaced by another form, a child care subsidy. A policy that deals with the direct cause of welfare dependence—low skills—would be more appropriate. There is no evidence that child care subsidies will increase economic self-sufficiency, defined as nonparticipation in means-tested government programs. Employment-related child care subsidies for middle-class families are even harder to rationalize.

The new welfare system created by the Personal Responsibility and Work Opportunity Reconciliation Act of 1996 imposes employment requirements and time limits on receipt of cash benefits. In the context of this system, child care subsidies might appear to be quite sensible. If welfare recipients are forced to accept employment at low wages, child care subsidies can help make employment more financially rewarding than cash assistance. But other policies, such as the EITC, can accomplish this as well, without the unintended consequences caused by employment-related child care subsidies such as low-quality child care. There is no logical connection between requiring employment and providing child care subsidies: if employment is to be required and if employment at typical jobs available to low-skilled individuals provides less net income than cash assistance, then a wage subsidy such as the EITC is a more direct remedy that does not induce distortions in child care incentives.

I question the wisdom of a welfare system that requires employment for mothers of young children, given the absence of evidence that this will lead to long-run economic independence, defined as not being dependent on *any* means-tested transfer, not just cash assistance. If child care subsidies and other employment-conditioned subsidies such as the EITC are necessary to make employment more financially rewarding than cash assistance, and if employment at low-skill jobs fails to lead to improved skills and wages, then why require employment? However, the main point I want to make here does not depend on the nature of the welfare system. The point is that employment-conditioned child care subsidies cannot be justified by the claim that the child care market is inefficient. The child care market may very well be inefficient, but not for reasons associated with employment.

It may be argued that equity considerations can justify intervention in the child care market. The poor have less money to spend on child care than others and are therefore likely to end up with lower-quality care in the absence of government intervention. This argument is not specific to child care: the poor are likely to end up with lower quality medical care, education, food, shelter, and other things that might affect child development. The problem is that the poor do not have enough money, not that they do not have enough money to afford high-quality child care. The government could, of course, provide subsidies to the poor for all of the goods and services deemed essential to healthy child development, and this is in fact the basis of most government policy toward the poor (Medicaid, food stamps, housing subsidies, and so forth). It would be simpler to transfer cash to the poor instead of subsidizing many different goods and services, but many people worry that the poor cannot be trusted to spend the cash on items deemed essential for the well-being of their children.

A PROPOSAL FOR REFORM

There are four elements to my proposal.[8] I describe these in general terms and then discuss the cost of the proposal based on a specific set of numbers for benefit levels, including savings from eliminating some existing programs. The goals of the proposal are to increase consumer knowledge about the benefits of high-quality child care, encourage consumers to use high-quality child care, encourage providers to offer high-quality care, and provide increased flexibility to parents of young children in making choices about employment. The proposal is tailored specifically to accomplish these goals, but I cannot offer any reliable evidence about how effective the program would be. Below, I present some illustrative calculations of take-up and cost based on my best guesses.

Provide a means-tested child allowance. Each family would receive an allowance from the federal government for up to two children, from birth through age 17. The allowance could take the form of a refundable tax credit, requiring that a family must file a tax return to claim the allowance. Refundability means that a family with no tax liability is eligible for the credit, so it is of value to low-income families. The value of the allowance should decline as the level of family income rises, and it should be phased out entirely for high-income families. There would be no restrictions on use of the allowance, since it would be in the form of cash. It could be used to pay for child care, food, housing, medical care, or other items that directly benefit children, but it could just as easily be used for other purposes. It could be used to subsidize non-employment by one of the parents, so that the parent can stay home to care for the child. It could also be used to pay for child care should parents choose to be employed. The principle behind a cash allowance is that parents care about the well-being of their children and are in the best position to decide how to allocate additional resources to improve child well-being. This feature of my proposal is very similar to Walker's (1996) proposed child allowance. I suggest that the allowance should be limited to two children per family in order to avoid providing strong pronatalist incentives.

Subsidize the cost of accreditation to child care providers. Organizations such as the National Association for the Education of Young Children (NAEYC) charge a fee to day care centers and preschools that seek to become accredited as high-quality providers. Organizations such as the NAEYC should be subsidized to provide accreditation services to child care providers at low or zero cost to the providers. A system with two levels of accreditation seems sensible to me, so that centers that are unable to qualify for the highest level of accreditation could nevertheless be certified as providing care of good quality by meeting an intermediate set of standards. In the system I have in mind, each provider would be either 1) unaccredited, meaning that it is not certified as offering high-quality care, though it presumably meets state regulatory standards; 2) accredited as offering care of good quality; or 3) accredited as offering care of excellent quality. Participation by providers would be voluntary; a provider that does not wish to become accredited is not required to do so. A similar system for family day care homes is feasible as well. However, baby-sitters and relatives would not be included in such a rating system. As discussed below, providers will have an incentive to offer high-quality child care and to be accredited as such.

Inform all new parents of the benefits of high-quality child care, how to recognize high-quality care, and how to find it. The simplest way to accomplish this would be to give a booklet and video with such information to mothers when they are in the hospital to give birth. The booklet and video should describe and illustrate in vivid terms what a high-quality child care arrangement looks and feels like, and contrast it with a low-quality arrangement. The consequences for child development of high- and low-quality care should be described, without making claims that cannot be supported by scientific evidence. The booklet and video should describe the accreditation system and should emphasize that accreditation is certified by independent agencies. They should also contain information on how to contact local resource and referral agencies and other sources of information about the local child care market.

Provide a means-tested child care voucher with a value that depends on the quality of the child care provider at which it is redeemed. The voucher would be worth more if it is used at an accredited provider. For example, a low-income family might receive a subsidy of 30 percent of the average cost of unaccredited child care, 60 percent of the average cost of "good quality" care, and 100 percent of the average cost of "excellent quality" care. This gives families an incentive to seek care of high quality, and it gives providers an incentive to offer high-quality care in order to attract consumers. The value of the voucher would be smaller for higher-income families, and it would be phased out entirely at high-income levels. The voucher would be of no value if the family does not purchase child care or pays a relative or baby-sitter for child care. This is a disadvantage, but it is unavoidable if the system is to contain incentives for the use of high quality care. Parents who do not use the voucher still receive benefits from the child allowance part of the system. The voucher does not require employment, so it would encourage use of high-quality care by non-employed mothers to enhance child development.

This proposed system is consistent with all of the principles described in the previous section. All of the elements of the system are neutral with respect to employment, consistent with freedom of parental choice, and rely on incentives rather than regulations. The child allowance and voucher make the system progressive, providing greater benefits for low-income families. The voucher and technical assistance subsidies provide incentives for improving quality of care demanded and supplied. The information booklet provides parents with the information needed to help them make well-informed decisions.

This proposed system would replace the entire current federal child care subsidy system. Employment-related child care subsidies, includ-

ing the DCTC, EEPDCE, the CCDF, and TXX-CC, would be eliminated. Head Start and Title I-A programs could be integrated into the
new system. These programs would be evaluated and accredited (or
not) by the same standards as other programs and would be eligible for
vouchers accordingly. Funding for these programs would be integrated
into the new subsidy system. Head Start and Title I-A establishments
could choose to maintain their special status as being designated
mainly for children from low-income families, or they could choose to
accept other children as well. The system would also replace all current tax deductions and credits for children, including the exemption
for children and the child tax credit. The proposed child allowance
serves the same purpose as these programs, so they would be redun-
dant. Finally, the proposed new system would also replace Temporary
Assistance for Needy Families (TANF). TANF provides cash assistance to low income families with children, and the child allowance
portion of my proposal does the same; however, my proposal does not
replicate the employment requirements and time limits of TANF. This
is a deliberate choice: though the child allowance benefit that I propose
is means-tested, the child allowance is not welfare and is phased out at
a relatively high level of income. Other policies could be used to
encourage employment of low-income parents if this is considered
desirable.

Because the proposed system is neutral with respect to employment, it would not replace programs that are explicitly intended to
encourage employment, such as the EITC, job training, and education
programs. If society considers it desirable for low-income single
mothers to be employed rather than receive cash assistance, the
voucher part of the child care system I propose provides considerable
resources that such mothers could use for child care. On the other
hand, the child allowance is likely to have a negative effect on employment, since this benefit would be available regardless of employment
status. So, unlike the current child care system, the proposed new system does not encourage employment, and if such encouragement is
desired it would have to come from another source.

The cost of the proposed new child care policy depends on a number of factors that are difficult to quantify, so the estimates I present
here are no more than illustrative. I try to justify the specific numbers
used in the calculations, but there is a large amount of unavoidable

arbitrariness. Hence these estimates are no more than educated guesses and should not be treated as reliable. I propose a child allowance of $5,000 per child aged 0–17 per year for families below the poverty line; $3,500 per child aged 0–17 for families with income between one and two times the poverty line; $2,000 per child aged 0–17 for families with income between two and four times the poverty line; and no allowance for families with income over four times the poverty line. The allowance would be provided for, at most, two children per family. Table 3 displays the average family income of each of these four income groups in 1999, and the numbers of children by age in each income group. The figures in the last three rows of the table show the number of eligible children, accounting for the maximum of two per family.

Table 4 shows illustrative cost calculations, based on the data in Table 3 and the figures assumed for the value of the voucher. The first two rows of Table 4 show the annual cost of the child allowance, assuming that all eligible children receive it. This cost is $131.608 billion.

The base amount of the proposed child care voucher is $6,000 for one preschool-aged child in a low-income family that redeems the voucher at a day care center accredited as providing high-quality care. This figure is an estimate of the cost of providing day care in a high-quality center. I used the "Cost, Quality, and Outcomes" data (Helburn 1995) to compute the average cost of care per child in day care centers with an Early Childhood Environment Rating Scale score of good or better (5–7 on a scale of 1–7). This was approximately $5,000 in 1993.[9] After adjusting for inflation, this amounts to $5,765 in 1999. I add an extra $235 per child to account for the higher real salary that will be needed to attract substantial numbers of well-qualified providers into the field. The $6,000 figure I use here can be compared to the $6,000 estimate of the cost of high-quality care used by Barnett (1993), which is equivalent to $6,918 after adjusting for inflation, and to the $5,417 cost per child of Head Start in 1998.[10] The value of the voucher is adjusted down by one-third for good quality care and by two-thirds for child care that is unaccredited. The value of the voucher is reduced by one-sixth for families between one and two times the poverty line and by one-half for families between two and four times the poverty

Table 3 Number of Children and Average Income, by Income/Needs Category

	I/N < 1.0	1.0 ≤I/N<2.0	2.0 ≤I/N<4.0	4.0 ≤ I/N
Average family income	$7,911	$23,800	$46,516	$108,350
All children				
Number of children				
< 6	4.688	4.854	7.085	5.539
6–12	5.499	6.146	9.554	7.337
13–17	2.932	3.565	6.511	5.965
Maximum of 2 children aged 0–12 per family				
Number of children				
< 6	4.402	4.683	6.911	5.443
6–12	3.829	4.808	8.169	6.596
Maximum of 2 children aged 0–17 per family				
Number of children				
0–17	9.919	11.938	20.115	17.759

NOTE: I/N is Income/Needs, total family income divided by the poverty standard for the size and structure of the family. Numbers of children are in millions. The figures under "Maximum of 2 children aged 0–12 per family" were computed as follows: if there were at least two children < 6, then number of children < 6 was set to two and number of children 6–12 was set to zero. If there was one child < 6 and at least one child 6–12, then the number < 6 and the number 6–12 were both set to one. If there were no children < 6 and at least two children 6–12, then the number of children 6–12 was set to two.

SOURCE: Tabulations from the March 1999 Current Population Survey.

Table 4 Illustrative Cost Calculations for a Proposed New Child Care System

	Family income needs ratio				Total cost
	0.0–1.0	1.01–2.0	2.01–4.0	4.01+	($, billions)
Allowance per child 0–17 ($)	5,000	3,500	2,000	0.0	
Cost of the child allowance, maximum of two children per family ($, billions)	49.595	41.783	40.230	0.0	131.608
Child care voucher per child <6 ($)					
High quality	6,000	5,000	3,000	0.0	
Good quality	4,000	3,333	2,667	0.0	
Other	2,000	1,667	1,333	0.0	
Child care voucher per child 6–12 ($)					
High quality	2,000	1,667	1,000	0.0	
Good quality	1,333	1,111	850	0.0	
Other	667	556	440	0.0	
Estimated number of voucher users (max. 2 per family) with children aged 0–5 (millions)					
High quality	2.861	3.044	4.492		
Good quality	0.660	0.702	1.037		
Other	0.440	0.468	0.691		
Estimated number of voucher users (max. 2 per family) with children aged 6–12 (millions)					
High quality	2.489	3.125	5.310		
Good quality	0.574	0.721	1.225		
Other	0.383	0.481	0.817		
Total cost of vouchers ($, billions)	26.685	24.617	23.873	0.0	75.176
Technical assistance					0.075
Information booklet and video					0.035
Gross total cost of the child care system					206.894

(continued)

Table 4 (continued)

	Family income needs ratio				Total cost
	0.0–1.0	1.01–2.0	2.01–4.0	4.01+	($, billions)
Savings from eliminating ($, billions):					
TANF	30.4				30.4
Child care subsidies					21.0
Tax exemption for dependent children	0	6.008	17.800	14.500	38.3
Child tax credit					21.6
Total savings					111.3
Net total cost of the child care system					95.594

NOTE: Assumes that 65% of eligible children will be in high quality child care, 15% in good quality care, 10% in other care, and 10% not in child care (and therefore not using the voucher). The cost calculations for technical assistance and information distribution are described in the text. TANF cost is computed from Administration for Children and Families (2000b) and includes state and federal cost. Child care subsidies are from Table 2, assuming items that are not available for 1999 are the same in 1999 as in the most recent year for which they are available. Savings from eliminating the tax exemption for children uses the deduction from income of $2750 per child, and assumes that families in poverty pay no income tax, families between one and two times the poverty line are in the 15% tax bracket, and other families are in the 28% bracket. Child tax credit figure is from Committee on Ways and Means (1998, p. 840).

line. It is reduced by two-thirds for children aged 6–12. Table 4 illustrates these adjustments.

The most speculative part of the calculation is estimating the take-up rate of the voucher. I have no sound basis for doing this, so my estimates are completely arbitrary. I assume that within each income group 65 percent of eligible children will use high-quality care, 15 percent will use good-quality care, 10 percent will use unaccredited care, and 10 percent will use no child care and therefore will not redeem the voucher. The value of the voucher to low-income families is quite high compared with existing subsidies (except for Head Start), so it seems sensible to assume that it will have a high take-up rate. For the other eligible income groups, I assume that the lower value of the voucher is compensated by higher income, and that the information dissemination part of the program convinces families to use high-quality care in large numbers. This is plausible because the value of the voucher is much higher than current child care subsidies available to families in the low- to middle-income range. Table 4 shows the implied cost of the vouchers: $75.176 billion. The costs of the other two parts of the system are minuscule compared with the cost of the allowance and the voucher. These are shown in Table 2 and amount to $110 million.[11]

The total cost of the proposed new system is $206.894 billion per year. However, as shown in Table 4, eliminating programs that would be redundant with the new system saves almost $111.3 billion per year. After accounting for savings due to eliminating TANF, child care subsidies, the tax exemption for dependent children, and the child tax credit, the net annual cost of the new system is $95.594 billion. This is obviously a very large sum and may not be politically feasible. Readers who have trouble swallowing a cost this large can use the information in Table 3 to compute the cost of child allowance and voucher subsidies of smaller magnitudes or with lower assumed take-up rates. The proposed system is highly progressive, but it does provide substantial benefits up to an income level of four times the poverty line, which is about $64,000 on average in 1999. Hence benefits are spread quite far up the income distribution, and about 75 percent of all children would be eligible for subsidies, based on the figures in Table 3. Assuming that the additional taxes needed to finance the cost of the system are raised in proportion to the current distribution of the income tax burden by income group, the system would be highly progressive. Other possibilities for reducing the net cost of the system would be to eliminate some other means-tested programs for families with children, such as food stamps and subsidized housing. I do not pursue this possibility here because I want to keep the focus on programs that are specifically child oriented.

The main losers under the proposed system are high-income families, who will lose the tax exemption, child care tax credit, and exclusion of employer-provided dependent care expenses with nothing gained in return. (See Blau 2001a, Chapter 10, for details.) In my judgment, these families can afford this loss with little hardship and would still be able to purchase child care of high quality. I have no objection in principle to providing benefits to all families regardless of income, but a universal system is far more expensive than a means-tested system, particularly if the value of the voucher and child allowance is not reduced at higher income.

There are many practical issues that would arise if such a system were to be implemented. Here I briefly discuss only three of these issues. First, how does the voucher get delivered to eligible families? The voucher is means-tested, but three-quarters of all children would be eligible, so it seems unlikely that stigma associated with use of a voucher would be a significant deterrent to its use. Nevertheless, because the child care subsidy is not universal, the voucher must somehow be delivered to eligible families, and there could be significant time costs to a family of securing a voucher. One possibility that could help avoid this is for the voucher to be delivered to families by the Internal Revenue Service, based on the tax return for the previous calendar year, and on an estimate by the family of changes in income and eligibility for the subsequent year. After filing a tax return for calendar year $t - 1$ in, say, March of year t, the family receives from the IRS in April a child care voucher for year t with a value based on calendar year $t - 1$ income, the age distribution of children anticipated in year t, and any adjustments to expected calendar year t income and age distribution of children noted by the family on the tax return. If income for year t turns out to be different than anticipated, the value of the voucher for the following year can be adjusted accordingly. The voucher is redeemed by the family at the chosen provider, and the provider returns it to a designated government office for compensation. This may require the provider and/or consumer to extend credit temporarily.

A second practical issue is the possibility of a shortage of high-quality child care during the transition to the new system. If tens of millions of families receive substantial new child care subsidies targeted for use in high-quality child care, the child care market may not be able to respond quickly with large increases in capacity. One way to make the transition smooth is to delay the distribution of vouchers until about a year after the new system becomes law, in order to give centers and family day care homes time to expand and upgrade quality. Any shortages that are caused by implementation of the new system are likely to be transitory, since providers will have strong incentives to expand capacity and upgrade quality in order to attract consumers with vouchers.

A final issue that should be discussed is the relationship between the proposed new system and state and local child care policy. The current child care subsidy system gives states some flexibility in how they use federal CCDF and TXX-CC subsidies, both of which are disbursed as block grants. States can choose the income eligibility criterion, the sliding-scale fee, and other features of their CCDF-funded programs, within limits. There is much less flexibility in the Head Start and Title I-A programs, since these must meet the uniform federal Head Start standards and income eligibility guidelines. States would lose some flexibility in the new system, because both the income eligibility and quality guidelines would be uniform federal standards. In fact, state bureaucracies that administer federally funded child care subsidies would no longer be needed, since all subsidies would be disbursed through the federal income tax system. However, many states have their own child care subsidy programs funded entirely by state funds. The proposed new system would not interfere with these programs. These programs vary widely, ranging from state child care tax credits and mini-CCDF-style programs, to teacher training initiatives and quality-improvement subsidies.[12] States would be free to fund whatever child care programs they like, or to discontinue such programs if they are found to be no longer necessary as a result of the expanded federal system.

CONCLUSION

Child care is a problem in the United States because the quality of care is low on average. Current child care policy does relatively little to address the problem because most child care subsidies are designed to encourage employment rather than enhance child development. The tension between these alternative goals ensures that debate and discussion of child care policy issues will continue for the foreseeable future. There is not a consensus on the goals of child care policy or on the means to achieve those goals. This is due in part to conflicting views on the proper role of the government in a domain that was mainly left to families as recently as a generation ago. My proposal is squarely on the side of enhancing child development, and this will no doubt be controversial. The proposal is quite costly, though it is possible to reduce the cost as much as desired by providing less generous subsidies. In exchange for the substantial cost of the proposal, one would hope for large benefits. I believe that there would be large benefits in the form of enhanced child development, leading to improved school performance, a more productive labor force, and fewer social problems such as crime and welfare dependence. But I cannot provide any compelling quantitative evidence to support this belief. In any case, most readers would probably like or dislike the proposal based on their values and beliefs rather than on evidence about its benefits and costs, even if reliable evidence were available. This is not offered as an excuse for the absence of evidence, but in recognition that there are limits to the ability of economic analysis to influence decision making.

Notes

Thanks to Jean Kimmel for comments. Comments welcome at david_blau@unc.edu.

1. The federal government does not have the authority to regulate child care; this is the responsibility of states. Child care regulations are an important part of the overall structure of government child care policy, but they are not discussed here because they are not part of federal child care policy. See Blau (2001b) and Blau (2001a, Chapter 8) for analysis of child care regulations.

2. Some smaller programs omitted from the table are listed in U.S. General Accounting Office (1994) and Robins (1991). A number of states have their own tax credits for child care, but they generally provide small benefits.

3. The programs were Aid to Families with Dependent Children—Child Care, Transitional Child Care, At-Risk Child Care, and the Child Care Block Grant. See Blau (in press) for details.

4. TANF is the cash assistance welfare program created by PRWORA in 1996 to replace AFDC.

5. Head Start served 822,316 children in FY1998, compared to an estimated 4.775 million children under age six in poverty in calendar year 1998 (Current Population Report P60-207, Table 2). However, 96 percent of children in Head Start are aged 3–5. Assuming that half the children under age six are aged 3–5 yields 34.4 percent as the percentage of 3- to 5-year-old children in poverty who are served by Head Start.

6. It is sometimes argued that shortages of child care of certain types in specific locations are important enough to justify government intervention. I do not believe this is a significant enough issue to warrant systematic government intervention. See Blau (2001a) for discussion of shortages in the child care market. Another argument for government child care subsidies is based on distributional considerations related both to cross-sectional equity at a given time and to the

long-run benefits to children of high-quality child care. Bergmann (1996, p. 131) argues that high-quality child care can be thought of as a "merit good, something that in our ethical judgment everybody should have, whether or not they are willing or able to buy it." In its pure form this argument is based solely on the moral grounds that it is unethical to deprive any child of the optimum conditions for development if society has the resources to provide such conditions.

7. Regulations can deal with information problems to some extent, by ensuring that all providers offer care of some minimum quality. This is discussed in Blau (2001a, Chapter 8).

8. Other proposals for reform of child care policy include Barnett (1993), Bergmann (1996), Gormley (1995), Helburn and Bergmann (2002), Kagan and Cohen (1996), Robins (1990), Walker (1996), and Zigler and Finn-Stevenson (1999). Gomby et al. (1996), Hayes, Palmer, and Zaslow (1990, Chapter 10), and Kahn and Kamerman (1987) also offer some suggestions for reform. See Blau (in press) for discussion of these proposals. I have borrowed liberally from these authors.

9. The cost figure includes the imputed value of donated space and volunteer labor.

10. Head Start Fact Sheet: http://www3.acf.dhhs.gov/programs/hsb/research/ 99_hsfs.htm.

11. The cost of accreditation is assumed to be $1,000, which is the maximum fee charged by the NAEYC for the accreditation process (http://www.naeye.org/ accreditation/default.asp). This is incurred every three years. In 2000 there were an estimated 106,000 licensed day care centers (The Children's Foundation 2000). I arbitrarily assume that there will be 150,000 day care centers in the new system, 50,000 of which would incur the accreditation cost per year, at $50 million. I arbitrarily add another $25 million per year for accreditation of family day care homes. I do not provide any direct subsidies for centers to improve their quality in order to satisfy the accreditation standards. I assume that centers will find it worthwhile to improve quality because of the large increase in demand for high-quality care prompted by the vouchers. Finally, the cost of producing and distributing the informational booklet and video are estimated at $10 per child, with an estimated 3.5 million children born per year.

12. See http://cpmcnet.columbia.edu/dept/nccp/main5.html and http:// www.gao.gov.news.items/he0011.pdf for information about state child care initiatives.

References

Adams, Gina, Karen Schulman, and Nancy Ebb. 1998. *Locked Doors: States Struggling to Meet the Child Care Needs of Low-Income Working Families*. Children's Defense Fund, Washington D.C., March.

Administration for Children and Families. 1998. "HHS Fact Sheet: State Spending Under the Child Care Block Grant." Http://www.acf.dhhs.gov/news/press/1998/cc97fund.htm, Washington D.C.

————. 1999. "Access to Child Care for Low-Income Working Families." Http://www.acf.dhhs.gov/news/press/1999/cc98.htm.Washington D.C.

————. 2000a. "New Statistics Show Only Small Percentage of Eligible Families Receive Child Care Help." Available at www.acf.2hhs.gov/news/press/2000/ccsxxx.hum.

————. 2000b. "TANF Program: Third Annual Report to Congress." Http://acf.dhhs.gov/opre/annual3-pdf, August.

Barnett, W. Steven. 1993. "New Wine in Old Bottles: Increasing Coherence in Early Childhood Care and Education Policy." *Early Childhood Research Quarterly* 8(4): 519–558.

Bergmann, Barbara. 1996. *Saving Our Children from Poverty: What the United States Can Learn from France.* New York: Russell Sage Foundation.

Blau, David M.. In press. "Child Care Subsidy Programs." In *Means-Tested Transfer Programs in the U.S.*, Robert Moffitt, ed. Chicago: University of Chicago Press.

————. 2001a. *The Child Care Problem: An Economic Analysis.* New York: The Russell Sage Foundation.

————. 2001b. "Do Child Care Regulations Affect the Child Care and Labor Markets?" Working paper.

The Children's Foundation. 2000. *The 2000 Child Care Licensing Study.* Washington D.C.

Committee on Ways and Means, U.S. House of Representatives. 1998. *1998 Green Book.* Washington D.C., May.

————. 2000. *2000 Green Book.* Washington, D.C., May.

Council of Economic Advisers. 1997. *The Economics of Child Care.* Washington, D.C.

Cryer, Debbie, and Margaret Burchinal. 1995. "Parents as Child Care Consumers." In *Cost, Quality, and Child Outcomes in Child Care Centers, Technical Report,* Suzanne W. Helburn, ed. Denver: Department of Economics, Center for Research in Economic and Social Policy, University of Colorado at Denver, June.

Currie, Janet. 2001. "Early Childhood Intervention Programs: What Do We Know?" *Journal of Economic Perspectives* 15(2): 213–238.

Gladden, Tricia, and Christopher Taber. 2000. "Wage Progression Among Less Skilled Workers." In *Finding Jobs: Work and Welfare Reform*, David Card and Rebecca Blank, eds. New York: Russell Sage Foundation, pp. 160–192.

Gomby, Deanna S., Nora Krantzler, Mary B. Larner, Carol S. Stevenson, Donna L. Terman, and Richard E. Behrman. 1996. "Financing Child Care: Analysis and Recommendations." *The Future of Children* 6(2): 5–25.

Gormley, William T. 1995. *Everybody's Children: Child Care as a Public Problem.* Washington, D.C.: The Brookings Institution.

Harms, Thelma, and Richard Clifford. 1980. *Early Childhood Environment Rating Scale.* New York: Teacher's College Press.

Hayes, Cheryl D., John L. Palmer, and Martha L. Zaslow. 1990. *Who Cares for America's Children? Child Care Policy for the 1990s.* Washington, D.C.: National Academy Press.

Helburn, Suzanne W. 1995. *Cost, Quality and Child Outcomes in Child Care Centers, Technical Report.* Department of Economics, University of Colorado at Denver.

Helburn, Suzanne W., and Barbara R. Bergmann. 2002. *America's Child Care Problem: The Way Out.* New York: Palgrave for St. Martin's Press.

Internal Revenue Service. 2001. "Tax Statistics: Individual Tax Statistics." *Complete Report Publication, Tax Year 1999.* Available on the Internet at http://www.irs.gov/taxstats.

Joint Committee on Taxation, U.S. Congress. 1999. "Estimates of Federal Tax Expenditures for Fiscal Years 2000–2004." Committee Print JCS-99, December 22, Washington, D.C.: U.S. Government Printing Office.

Kagan, Sharon L., and Nancy Cohen. 1996. "A Vision for a Quality Early Care and Education System." In *Reinventing Early Care and Education: A Vision for a Quality System,* Sharon Kagan and Nancy Cohen, eds. San Francisco: Jossey-Bass, 304–332.

Kahn, Alfred, and Shiela Kamerman. 1987. *Child Care: Facing the Hard Choices.* Dover, Massachusetts: Auburn House.

Karoly, Lynn A., Peter W. Greenwood, Susan S. Everingham, Jill Houbé, M. Rebecca Kilburn, C. Peter Rydell, Matthew Sanders, and James Chiesa. 1998. *Investing in Our Children: What We Know and Don't Know About the Costs and Benefits of Early Childhood Interventions.* RAND Report MR-898-TCWF, Santa Monica, California.

Magenheim, Ellen B. 1995. "Information, Prices, and Competition in the Child Care Market: What Role Should Government Play?" In *Readings in Public Policy,* J.M. Pogodzinksi, ed. Cambridge, Massachusetts: Blackwell, pp. 269–307.

Office of Management and Budget. 1996. *Budget of the United States Government, Fiscal Year 1997,* Washington, D.C.: OMB.

Robins, Philip K. 1990. "Federal Financing of Child Care: Alternative Approaches and Economic Implications." *Population and Policy Review* 9(January): 65–90.

———. 1991. "Child Care Policy and Research: An Economist's Perspective." In *The Economics of Child Care*, David Blau ed. New York: Russell Sage Foundation.

Sonenstein, F. L. 1991. "The Child Care Preferences of Parents with Young Children." In *Parental Leave and Child Care: Setting a Research and Policy Agenda,* J. S. Hyde and M. J. Essex, eds. Philadelphia: Temple University Press, pp. 337–353.

U.S. Department of Agriculture. 2001. *Child and Adult Care Food Program.* Available at www.fns.usda.gov/cnd/care.

U.S. Department of Education. 1996. "Policy Guidance for Title I, Part A: Improving Basic Programs Operated by Local Educational Agencies." Available on the Internet at http://www.ed.gov/legislation/ESEA/Title_I/preschoo.html.

U.S. Department of Labor. 1998. Issues in Labor Statistics. Summary 98-9, Washington, D.C., August.U.S. General Accounting Office. 1994. *Early Childhood Programs: Multiple Programs and Overlapping Target Groups.* Report GAO/HEHS-95-4FS, Washington D.C., October.

———. 1998. *Welfare Reform: States' Efforts to Expand Child Care Programs.* Report GAO/HEHS-98-27, Washington D.C., January.

———. 1999. *Early Education and Care: Early Childhood Programs and Services for Low-Income Families.* Report GAO/HEHS-00-11, Washington D.C., November.

———. 2000a. *Child Care: State Efforts to Enforce Safety and Health Requirements.* Report GAO/HEHS-00-28, Washington D.C., January.

———. 2000b. *Title I Preschool Education: More Children Saved but Gauging Effect on School Readiness Difficult.* Report GAO/HEHS-00-171. Washington, D.C., September.

Walker, James. 1991. "Public Policy and the Supply of Child Care Services." In *The Economics of Child Care*, David Blau, ed. New York: Russell Sage Foundation.

———. 1996. "Funding Child Rearing: Child Allowance and Parental Leave." *The Future of Children* 6(2): 122–136.

Zigler, Edward, and Matia Finn-Stevenson. 1999. *Schools of the Twenty-First Century: Linking Child Care and Education.* Boulder, Colorado: Westview Press.

2
Thinking about Child Care Policy

Barbara R. Bergmann
Professor Emerita, American University
and the University of Maryland

Two revolutions in the latter half of the twentieth century have changed the way our society finances and arranges for the care and rearing of young children. One is women's entry into the labor market; almost two-thirds of mothers with children under six are now in the paid workforce. The second revolution, which resulted from the same economic and social developments as the first, is the increase in the number of single-parent families; they now constitute about one-quarter of the families with children under 6, and they tend to have much lower incomes than other types of families (U.S. Bureau of Labor Statistics 2000). These two revolutions make the traditional model of providing and financing child care—an at-home wife supported by a bread-winning husband—no longer useful for the care of most children.

We have yet to face up to the implications and requirements of those enormously important changes. The paychecks of mothers—both married and single—are now an important source of support for millions of families. In a growing number of cases they are an indispensable source of support. Yet the high cost of child care makes severe inroads on those paychecks and therefore on the standard of living of families. Child care costs can take away 25 percent or more of the incomes of low-wage families.[1] And millions of children are not getting the quality of care that would do justice to their needs for safety, nurture, and development.

The kind of care children receive, as well as the cost of that care and its effect on a family's standard of living, are issues that deserve—and are beginning to receive—national attention. The high cost of child care is one of the major causes of low living standards, lack of self-support, and social pathology in families with children. Obviously, that is, or should be, a matter of public concern. The low quality of care that many young children receive should also be of public concern, as it affects the kind of adult population we will have in the future—it affects the psychological security, the social maturity, and the economic productivity of the future citizens of this country. Equally important, the kind of care a child receives affects the quality of his or her life right now in regard to feelings of happiness, security, and self-worth. The care children receive can also affect parents' ability to get to work reliably, and to feel secure that while at work their children are well cared for. This in turn affects worker productivity, labor turnover, and thus employers' costs of production.

If there is general agreement that child care in the United States is a serious problem, there is little agreement on what to do about it. Conservatives say mothers (with the exception of single mothers, perhaps) should stay home with their children. They regard the movement of mothers out of the home and into jobs as a terrible mistake, and believe that the lack of full-time care by mothers has produced cohorts of unsupervised, unhappy children, many of whom are without morals, are poorly socialized, and are prone to crime. A Republican leader in the U.S. House of Representatives, commenting on a massacre perpetrated by high school students, mentioned day care as a major cause.[2] Libertarians would rely totally on the free market to evolve a supply of care that would be appropriate to the country's needs in terms of quality and cost, and would favor withdrawing what government subsidies and regulations are now in place. Some people argue that government and employer help to families with children discriminates against the childless. Others present the contrary argument, that parents are aiding society by raising children and deserve society's help in doing so. Many advocates of that help look to community action, such as corporations, charities, and foundations, to mobilize the resources to improve the quality and availability of child care in each locality. There are others who hope that state and local governments will increasingly contribute to help parents with child care, and will address part of the problem through the increased provision of free pre-kindergartens. Finally, there are those, myself included, who believe that only a large, active, and expensive federal program, providing both finance and a national framework for quality improvement, will serve the nation's purposes adequately.

The welfare reform of 1996, whatever else it accomplished, forced a recognition of the fact that working mothers were here to stay, and that many of them needed and deserved help in obtaining care of decent quality for their children. It was accompanied by a considerable increase in federal and state funds devoted to paying for child care, but computed on any rational basis, the expansion has by no means been sufficient to fill the need. Current appropriations still cover only a small proportion of those eligible to receive help under present rules, to say nothing of those who are not now eligible but arguably should be.

COSTS AND PRICES

Full-time care for a child under five is a "big-ticket item." We can estimate that parents working full time paid an average of $7,777 per child for licensed care in a center in the year 2000. Those who used family day care, most of which is unlicensed and unregulated, paid an average of $6,413.[3] Some families had a relative who provided child care at no charge, but about one-third of relatives (other than fathers) charged for care. Even a middle-income family with two preschool-aged children in licensed care has a large financial burden.

The high price of child care is a crucial aspect of the "affordability" problem. For a large number of families, paying these prices means parting with a painfully large portion of their incomes. For some parents, the price of child care keeps them from working. Other parents put their children into affordable but low-quality care that is so poor, it may even bring harm. Still other parents use so much of their income for child care that they are unable to buy the basic goods and services they need to live decently.

Is the price of child care too high? The only prices that economists would characterize as too high occur in situations where competition is absent or weak, and where the price-setter can take advantage of the customers' lack of alternative sellers to raise prices far above costs. The child care industry is marked by vigorous competition and relative ease of entry for new competitors, so we do not see prices unreasonably elevated above costs. In the for-profit part of the industry, revenues are close to costs and the margin of profit is low. The nonprofits receive some help from government programs and private sources, but they, as well as the for-profit centers, depend heavily on fees to cover their costs. We can conclude that it would be impossible to reduce fees significantly by reducing profits or surpluses.

Could costs be reduced? Labor costs are 70 percent of the total cost of child care centers (Cost, Quality, and Child Outcomes Study Team 1995) and an even larger share of the cost of other modes of care. Child care inevitably takes a lot of labor time; providers cannot hope for the steady evolution of labor-saving machinery, which raises productivity and cuts cost through time in most other modern industries. (The only labor-saving machinery available for this industry is television, and its extensive use degrades the quality of care.) If child care providers try to economize on labor by giving care givers larger groups of children to supervise, quality will suffer. This is not to say that every child care center is optimally managed; undoubtedly some providers could achieve cost-savings through better management. However, the opportunities for lowering costs appear minor compared with the forces making for higher costs per child.

Prices for child care have been on an upward trend. Between 1990 and 2000, while the overall consumer price index was rising by 29 percent, fees child care centers and nursery schools charged were rising by 56 percent.[4] We can expect this upward trend in child care prices, relative to prices charged for other goods and services, to continue. As most other industries experience rising labor productivity over time, we can expect a resumption of the economy-wide upward trend in real wages which, until relatively recently, has been a long-run feature of Western economies. Rising wages will have an especially heavy impact on costs and prices in a labor-intensive industry such as child care. Upward changes in the legal minimum wage will also raise costs in child care relative to costs in other industries. Moreover, a successful campaign to improve child care quality would accentuate the rise in costs because it would require better trained and better paid workers.

Thus, when we talk about making child care affordable, we are not talking about reducing costs. On the contrary, costs are rising, and we can expect them to continue to rise over time, relative to the costs of most other goods and services. Whatever the inflation rate we have in the general level of prices, the rise in child care costs and prices is likely to exceed it by a considerable amount. So reducing child care costs is not something we can realistically hope to achieve through any sort of government policy. The only way to make child care affordable to families with children is to transfer the burden of some or all of those unavoidably high costs from parents to some other set of persons.

CHILD CARE AFFORDABILITY FOR FAMILIES MOST IN NEED

We now take a closer look at the question of affordability. The question is what amount constitutes affordable child care, and how much of the cost of child care should be born by public subsidies, given a family's size and financial circumstances. Obviously, reasonable people would differ on such a question. Nevertheless, by looking at particular cases it is possible to zero in on an idea of affordability which, if not meeting everybody's exact standard, would be considered reasonable by most people.

It makes sense to start our discussion of affordability with the simplest and most obvious case, that of a single mother, working full time at a minimum wage job. We will assume she has two children, ages one and three. She may never have been on welfare, or perhaps recently moved off. In the former case, she is likely getting no help at all in paying for child care from any current government program. The case of the low-wage single mother is not one that politicians find the most compelling. People like her don't vote in large numbers, and single mothers who need help are not popular with large segments of the American public. Arguably, her plight is likely to have been the result of unwise behavior: having children out of wedlock or having them within wedlock in a marriage headed for breakup. Nevertheless, hers is a good case to start with because her need is so stark, obvious, and understandable. And whatever her history, she is now working and thus "playing by the rules."

Obviously, a low-wage, single mother needs someone to care for her children while she works. Some people assume that the typical single mother has a relative who is willing to provide quality care for her children for free (Kaus 1992), but that is not the reality (Presser 1989). Currently about half of working single mothers do get free care, mostly from relatives,[5] although some of those arrangements are far from ideal. But the other half—those who must pay—is our main concern.

What is affordable child care for a family headed by a low-wage single woman? One obvious way to think about the family's ability to pay for child care is to see how much money the family takes in during a year, and how much it would cost to buy the goods and services (other than child care) that would provide a poverty-line standard of living. Out of her income the mother needs to pay taxes, buy adequate food, pay for housing, and see that other necessities such as transportation to work, clothing, and toiletries are paid for. We have left medical expenses out of the list because she is eligible for Medicaid. After accounting for these minimal necessities, we can see how much money is left over to cover the cost of providing care for the family's children. If the amount remaining is insufficient to buy care of an acceptable quality, then keeping this family at a poverty-line standard of living would require some form of government help to make child care affordable.

The financial situation of the family of our working single mother in the year 2000 is summarized in Table 1. The first panel of the table gives information on the amount of money the mother will have to live on. Working at the minimum wage of $5.15 for 40 hours a week, 52 weeks a year, would bring in $10,712 per year. To see how much money she will have available to spend—her disposable income—we subtract from her wage income the taxes the family owes and add in any benefits she will be entitled to. This family's income is too low to owe any federal or state income taxes, but it does pay Social Security taxes of $819. Offsetting this subtraction are several government benefits which families with an earned income this low are entitled to receive: the Earned Income Tax Credit (EITC) of $3,888 and food stamp benefits of $1,955. After these subtractions and additions, we arrive at a disposable income of $15,736.

The second panel of the table gives two alternative assessments of what a minimally decent standard of living would cost this family. The first is the official U.S. poverty line figure of $13,898. The poverty line is specified as the cost of a thrifty food budget multiplied by three. It is revalued yearly, to take account of price changes. The official poverty measure was set up in the early 1960s, when most families with children had a stay-at-home mother. Child care needs were thus

Table 1 Financial Situation of a Single Mother with Two
Preschool Children in a Full-Time, Minimum-Wage Job, 2000

Ability to spend	
Pre-tax wages[a]	$10,712
Federal and state income taxes	0
Earned income tax credit	3,888
Social security taxes	−819
Food stamps[b]	1,955
Disposable income	15,736
Minimum budget, excluding child care	
Official poverty line	$13,898
Required expenditure for food, clothing, shelter, transportation, and services[c]	15,587
Cost of child care[d]	
Center care for two children, ages 1 and 3	$13,460
For family day care	12,826

[a] Assumes work of 40 hours per week, 52 weeks per year at the 1998 minimum wage of $5.15.

[b] The family may be eligible to receive additional food stamps equal to 30 percent of expenditures on child care, up to a maximum of stamps worth $1,350 in a year. Food stamp benefits may also be increased for those paying relatively high rents.

[c] According to the National Academy of Sciences budget (exclusive of child care and health insurance).

[d] Derived from census data.

not allowed for, and it is reasonable to characterize the official poverty-line income as representing one estimate of the cost of a minimal budget, exclusive of child care costs.

The second assessment shown in the panel is based on the work of a committee of experts assembled by the National Academy of Sciences (NAS) in the early 1990s. By then, it was obvious that child care costs needed to be taken into account. The NAS experts concluded that there should be a new official poverty line based on a detailed family budget, rather than on the "food cost times three" calculation that has been used to calculate what is now the official poverty line.[6] The detailed budget provides a more realistic accounting for minimal needs for food, clothing, shelter, transportation, services, and taxes, better consideration of health care needs, and of the child care needs of employed parents.[7] One version of the NAS's minimal basic budget for a family of this composition, exclusive of taxes and health insurance and exclusive of child care costs, would come to $15,587 for the year 2000. The disposable income provided by the minimum wage and other benefits that a parent earning the minimum wage receives is just about par with the amount the NAS decided this three-person family needs to spend in order to have a poverty-line package of goods and services. To be precise, our sample mother would have $149 remaining after following the NAS budget.

The third panel in Table 1 gives two alternative amounts for the cost of care. The first is the average cost of full-time center care for two children, ages one and three, a total of $13,460.[8] The second alternative is the average cost of family child care, much of which is unregulated or unlicensed.

It is obvious that this mother can bear little of the burden of paying for child care. Her disposable income will virtually be exhausted in purchasing the goods and services needed for a poverty-line standard of living, whichever of the two poverty lines one adopts. What she has left over would finance only a fraction of the cost of caring for one child; it would certainly not cover the cost for the care of two, regardless of the form of care. If the family is required to divert anything but a small portion of its disposable income to pay for child care, it will be forced below a poverty-line standard of living. It seems reasonable, then, to say that the only affordable price this family can pay for child care is close to zero.

What is the rationale for government action to make child care affordable for this family? Action is clearly needed if our society wants to adhere to the principle that when people work and thus "play by the rules" in this richest of all countries, they should have a standard of living that meets some basic minimum and their children should have care of a decent quality. Of course, not everyone is willing to subscribe to the proposition that such a family ought to be helped with child care costs. Some argue that people whose income doesn't allow them to support children decently and pay for good quality care out of their own resources simply shouldn't have children. In this view, if they do have children, it is best if they (and the children) suffer the consequences; government help to them would merely encourage irresponsible behavior and dependency in themselves and others.

When considering both sides of this argument, it is important to remember that we are talking about a mother who works full time all year round at an unskilled job, perhaps cleaning offices or hotel rooms, who has nobody with whom to share family chores, and who is raising children who will be future citizens, future earners, and future taxpayers. Many of the nation's children live in families with characteristics similar to these. The question at hand is whether we as a nation want to insure that such children and their parents do not have a standard of life lower than the poverty line.

AFFORDABLE CHILD CARE FOR FAMILIES ABOVE THE LOWEST-EARNING BRACKET

We now go on to consider the situation of families with more than minimum-wage earnings who have no government help with child care costs. The single mother we have been using as an example would need a wage rate almost three times the minimum wage in order to live above the poverty-line level and pay the average price of care for her children without government assistance. Referring again to Table 1, we can see that she would have to spend $13,898 in order to buy the goods and services providing a standard of living at the official poverty level, and she would have to pay an additional $13,460 for child care. To be able to spend those sums she would need a disposable income in the year 2000 of $27,358.[9] To have a disposable income that large she would need to earn a wage of $29,655 because she would have to pay federal and state income taxes. (The figures quoted here are based on the state tax rates in Colorado.)[10] Only about 21 percent of single mothers earn that much; the median wage earned by single mothers who are employed was under $19,000 in that year.[11]

In Table 2, the results of this kind of calculation is shown for single parents and for couples with differing numbers and ages of children. We assume that preschoolers need full-time care and any school-age children need after-school and summer care. The table shows, for example, that a couple with four children would need almost $44,000

Table 2 Estimates of the Wage Income Required to Maintain a Poverty-Line Standard of Living and Pay for Child Care in a Center, for Families of Various Sizes and Compositions, 2000

Number of children		Family type and income characteristics					
		Poverty line ($)		Disposable income needed ($)		Pre-tax wage needed ($)	
Under 5	School-age	Single	Married	Single	Married	Single	Married
0	1	11,889	13,885	13,712	15,708	11,787	12,965
1	0	11,889	13,885	18,642	20,638	18,661	21,276
0	2	13,898	17,493	17,544	21,139	13,644	18,928
1	1	13,898	17,493	22,474	26,069	22,308	27,347
2	0	13,898	17,493	27,358	30,953	29,655	34,035
1	2	17,554	20,586	27,953	30,985	29,988	33,552
2	1	17,554	20,586	32,837	35,869	36,194	39,340
2	2	20,271	23,049	37,377	40,155	40,970	43,788

SOURCE: Computed by the author based on tax and benefit rates. The state tax formula used is that of Colorado. The care of children under 5 is assumed to cost the average amount indicated by the census survey of 1993. One child under 5 is assumed to be one year old. A second child under 5 is assumed to be three years old. The poverty lines for 2000 are based on those for 1999 updated by price changes through July 2000.

in wages to live at a poverty-line standard and afford center care for those under school age and after-school care for those in school. That means that a couple with four children who didn't have an income that large would have to choose between center care of average quality for their children and living at a standard below the poverty line. The table thus demonstrates in a simple way an important truth: parents with substantial middle-class incomes need help paying for child care if they are to have a standard of living that even comes up to that permitted by a poverty line income. As we shall see, there is a sensible argument for extending help with child care costs to families with wage incomes considerably above those indicated in Table 2.

A WORKABLE DEFINITION OF AFFORDABLE
CHILD CARE

The argument so far has demonstrated a simple proposition: if working families with children are to have living standards that at least come up to the poverty line, we need to provide child care subsidies to families with incomes considerably above the poverty line. There are three important characteristics to a program that provides affordable care.

First, families with incomes at or below the poverty line should pay little or nothing for child care. Families with incomes above the poverty line should be required to spend on child care only some fraction of the amount by which their income exceeds the poverty line. That would guarantee that working families with children would not have to endure a below-the-poverty-line standard of living because of child care costs. We believe this to be the core of any reasonable definition of affordability. Second, the subsidy paid out of government funds, together with the co-payment required of the parents, should be enough to buy care of a respectable quality. Finally, if the subsidies for child care are phased out for the higher-income groups, they should be phased out gradually. If a family's income rises, the subsidy to which it is entitled should not as a result decrease by even more, leaving the family worse off.[12]

Table 3 shows four variants of a subsidy plan that would have the characteristics we have laid out, as applied to a couple with one three-year-old child (Panel A), and to a couple with an infant and a three-year-old (Panel B). Families receiving the benefit would be required to make a co-payment at a rate equal to some percentage of their income above the poverty line. A family at or below the poverty line makes no co-payment and receives a benefit equal to the full cost of care. The table shows benefits under four different co-payment rates, ranging from 50 percent down to zero.[13] In Panel A, subsidies and parents' co-payments add up to $6,707, our estimate of what center care of average quality would cost for a three-year-old in the year 2000. In Panel B the cost of care for the two children would be $13,460.

What is our ideal co-payment rate? The answer depends on the extent to which we think taxpayers should help parents—particularly

Table 3 Annual Child Care Benefits and Co-Payments for Parents Choosing Center Care, under Four Rates of Co-Payment

	A. Benefits for a couple with one 4-year old ($)							
Rate of co-payment	50%		30%		20%		0%	
Income	Child care benefit	Parents pay	Child care benefit	Parents pay	Child care benefit	Parents pay	Child care benefit	Parents pay
10,000	6,707	0	6,707	0	6,707	0	6,707	0
15,000	6,150	558	6,373	335	6,484	223	6,707	0
20,000	3,650	3,058	4,873	1,835	5,484	1,223	6,707	0
25,000	1,150	5,558	3,373	3,335	4,484	2,223	6,707	0
30,000	0	6,707	1,873	4,835	3,484	3,223	6,707	0
35,000	0	6,707	373	6,335	2,484	4,223	6,707	0
40,000	0	6,707	0	6,707	1,484	5,223	6,707	0
45,000	0	6,707	0	6,707	484	6,223	6,707	0
50,000	0	6,707	0	6,707	0	6,707	6,707	0
55,000	0	6,707	0	6,707	0	6,707	6,707	0
60,000	0	6,707	0	6,707	0	6,707	6,707	0
65,000	0	6,707	0	6,707	0	6,707	6,707	0
70,000	0	6,707	0	6,707	0	6,707	6,707	0
75,000	0	6,707	0	6,707	0	6,707	6,707	0
80,000	0	6,707	0	6,707	0	6,707	6,707	0
85,000	0	6,707	0	6,707	0	6,707	6,707	0

B. Benefits for a couple with a 1-year old and a 3-year old ($)

10,000	13,460	0	13,460	0	13,460	0	13,460	0
15,000	13,460	0	13,460	0	13,460	0	13,460	0
20,000	12,207	1,254	12,708	752	12,959	501	13,460	0
25,000	9,707	3,754	11,208	2,252	11,959	1,501	13,460	0
30,000	7,207	6,254	9,708	3,752	10,959	2,501	13,460	0
35,000	4,707	8,754	8,208	5,252	9,959	3,501	13,460	0
40,000	2,207	11,254	6,708	6,752	8,959	4,501	13,460	0
45,000	0	13,460	5,208	8,252	7,959	5,501	13,460	0
50,000	0	13,460	3,708	9,752	6,959	6,501	13,460	0
55,000	0	13,460	2,208	11,252	5,959	7,501	13,460	0
60,000	0	13,460	708	12,752	4,959	8,501	13,460	0
65,000	0	13,460	0	13,460	3,959	9,501	13,460	0
70,000	0	13,460	0	13,460	2,959	10,501	13,460	0
75,000	0	13,460	0	13,460	1,959	11,501	13,460	0
80,000	0	13,460	0	13,460	959	12,501	13,460	0
85,000	0	13,460	0	13,460	0	13,460	13,460	0

middle-class parents—with the burden of child care costs. The co-payment rate determines how high the parents' incomes will be when the aid for child care goes down to zero. In Panel B of Table 2, a 50 percent co-payment rate cuts off aid to couples earning $45,000 or more, while a 20 percent rate extends aid to couples making almost $80,000.

The zero co-payment rate provides free care to all children, regardless of family income. This is the same provision that is made when children enter public school a few years later. Some countries subsidize considerable amounts of child care to the same extent they subsidize elementary and secondary schooling. For example, France provides free preschools for all children between two and six, run by the public school system. Care for the hours before and after school is available for modest fees (Bergmann 1996). The Canadian province of Quebec has a publicly subsidized child care system that provides care for $5 a day, regardless of the parents' income (Peritz 2000).

While there is no scientific answer to the question of which co-payment rate is best, there are some considerations pointing to a rate toward the low end of the spectrum. If the co-payment rate is higher, parents will receive less help and be more likely to ignore the subsidized programs and instead seek bargain-basement care from unlicensed providers. So a higher rate will on average result in lower-quality care for children. It would be good public policy to give parents an adequate incentive to use licensed care. Subsidies which pay part of the cost of care that is of better-than-minimally-acceptable quality do provide an incentive, especially if their use is restricted to providers that meet such quality standards. But subsidies that pay only a low share of the cost give only a weak incentive, especially for parents with low-to-middle incomes.

The co-payment can be thought of as a special tax the family pays, and it must be paid on top of the other taxes the family owes. Under a 50 percent co-payment rate, the family would retain a relatively minor share of its above-poverty spending power to use for its other living expenses; for that reason, and because of its harshness, we consider it much too high. The phaseout of benefits used in some state child care subsidy plans under the Child Care and Development Fund program (CCDF) is equivalent to a co-payment rate of about 30 percent. The phaseout of the EITC is equivalent to a rate of 16–20 percent. Couples with pre-tax income up to about $50,000 are taxed at 15 percent.

If co-payments are charged, the best case can be made for a rate no higher than 20 percent of income over the poverty line. Another reasonable configuration would be a modest flat fee of perhaps $5 a day per child, with rebates for families close to the poverty line. Obviously, there are other, more complicated designs that might serve.

SHOULD THE GOVERNMENT PAY?

Any adequate national child care program would involve a considerable increase in government spending for child care, on the order of tens of billions of dollars annually. Is this the only way it could be financed? Are there other sources of financing that might make major contributions? The attacks by conservatives on "big government" and on policies of "tax and spend" that have gone on since the 1970s have been very successful in conveying the idea that new high-cost public programs should never be considered, and that some of the ones we already have (particularly Social Security and the public schools, although not defense) are ripe for dismantlement. Furthermore, President Bill Clinton's statement that "The era of big government is over," appeared to put beyond the pale any ambitions for a public program of the type and magnitude we are advocating.

Those who believe that large new programs are unthinkable, or at least politically infeasible, have thus tended to look elsewhere (such as employers or charitable organizations) for aid in supplying affordable high-quality child care. It is unrealistic to think that charitable contributions to child care could suffice to make up a major share of the tens of billions of dollars needed—even if those contributions expanded tenfold, they would not begin to solve the financial problems.

Those despairing of a significant increase in government provision or subsidy of child care are also attracted to the idea that employers might take a prominent role in providing resources and organizing programs. There are several reasons why employers are thought of in this connection. There is the American tradition of providing for social needs like health insurance, sick leave, and vacations through employer-provided "fringe benefits," rather than through government programs, as is done in Europe. Child care centers located in workplaces offer important advantages such as convenience and contact during the work day between parents and children.

We need to ask whether it is realistic to expect employers to contribute much to solving the country's child care problems. There is no reason to believe that employers will voluntarily provide an appreciable share of the additional billions of dollars needed every year to finance good-quality child care, or that they could be forced to do it by legislation or cajoled into it by tax incentives. On the contrary, many employers are currently making big efforts to reduce their fringe benefits, largely by keeping some of their employees in a part-time status and making part-timers ineligible for benefits. Additionally, they are reducing the amounts they pay for the health insurance of full-time workers.

Even in the unlikely event that employer help with child care expenses were to become as common as employer help with health insurance, a lot of people would still be without coverage. We would be left with the same spotty picture we have today in health insurance, where the concept of transitioning from employer-coverage to universal coverage is increasingly more difficult and more complicated. In regard to child care, it is perhaps fortunate that employers provide as little help as they do.

TAX BREAKS VERSUS PROVIDER PAYMENTS AS A MODE OF FINANCE

A rationalized system of child care finance, especially for children under four, would concentrate on just one of the two modes of help we now have for parents with child care expenses—either the block grants to the states which finance payments to child care providers or the tax breaks which reimburse parent expenses—and eliminate the other. A one-mode system would be more efficient to operate and would make clearer the extent of the system's generosity and equity.

If one of the existing systems is to be expanded, which should it be? One possibility would be to expand the tax break mode we now use to finance child care help for the middle class and use it as the basis of a larger and more inclusive system of help to parents with child care expenses. That would mean increasing considerably the tax benefits available to lower-income families, and making the tax credits refundable.

It seems politically easier in the United States to provide social programs in the form of tax breaks than it is to get Congress to finance them by appropriations. Conservatives say that expenditures "spend the people's money," while tax breaks "give the money back to the people who earned it." However, this distinction is misleading. Tax breaks take money out of the treasury just as expenditures do; for this reason economists call them "tax expenditures." A dollar given to a provider to help a parent with child care fees benefits the parent and costs the government treasury no more or less than a dollar rebated to the parent by the tax authority, provided the restrictions on the parent's use of the dollar is the same in both cases.

Tax breaks are not limited by yearly appropriations. As a result, no one is turned away or put on a waiting list (as happens frequently to applicants for child care subsidies financed by the child care block grants or to applicants for housing benefits), because the amount that has been appropriated is insufficient to pay for the benefit for all those entitled to it. The entitlement aspect to benefits distributed through the tax system is certainly an advantage from the point of view of those who would like to see more expenditures on behalf of child care, and more equity in the distribution of those expenditures.

There are some important disadvantages to using the tax system to fund child care subsidies. First, the size of the subsidies that are needed for low-income families are large. A low-income family with three preschool children might require $20,000 a year or more in child care subsidies, and subsidies of this magnitude, so out of proportion to any taxes owed, would be awkward to distribute as a refundable tax break. Child care subsidies, especially those that cover a high proportion of the cost, need to be paid or reimbursed at least on a monthly basis, something the tax authorities are not in a good position to do. The administration of the EITC by the IRS has been troubled by a considerable number of fraudulent claims; the much larger amounts to be handed out in child care subsidies would make an even more tempting target for false claims.

Perhaps the most telling argument against depending on tax breaks as a financing mode relates to quality assurance. The IRS, as it is currently set up, is not equipped to pay attention to such things. A major purpose of a national child care program that would fund the considerable fees that licensed caregivers charge is that our children would be provided with good-quality care. That purpose would be nullified in a system that reimbursed fees to anybody with a Social Security number.

UNEARMARKED CASH BENEFITS

Conservatives who wish to encourage maternal care and discourage nonmaternal care tend to resist providing subsidies to paid care. They advocate instead cash benefits "for child care" that are not conditional on or earmarked for child care expenses.[14] The standard argument for them is that they give parents freedom to choose how they wish to care for their children. These unearmarked benefits are helpful to family budgets and are therefore useful in providing a better living standard for children. However, if they are set up as a total replacement for subsidies earmarked for nonmaternal child care, they are harmful because they lack a major characteristic of earmarked subsidies: encouraging parents to upgrade the quality of the care their children get. A family receiving an extra cash payment worth several thousand dollars labeled "for child care" but which they can spend any way they want, may spend some of it to improve their child's care. But they are unlikely to spend all of it, or even most of it, in this way. This is particularly true if the family has a low income and is lacking many of the goods and services commonly thought necessary to maintain a decent lifestyle. By contrast, a voucher worth several thousand dollars that can only be used to purchase licensed care may succeed in shifting a child from unlicensed care to licensed care.[15]

To drive the point home, we can draw the analogy to methods of giving health care benefits. The only way for children to be covered by health insurance is to have them signed up for health insurance, with the government payment going to the providers. Nobody would imagine that a $3,000 unearmarked payment "to help families buy their children health insurance" would have as much impact on the number of children covered, or on the quality of the coverage, as would the presentation to the family of a noncashable voucher for the health insurance itself.   Similarly, a $3,000 cash benefit that was sent in an envelope marked "to help the family pay its child care bills" would have much less impact on the quality or type of care that was bought by the family for the child than a voucher worth $3,000 which could only be used to pay part of child care bills.

THE COST OF MAKING CHILD CARE AFFORDABLE

A new national plan is needed that would build upon and go beyond our present system in terms of number of families helped and the degree of help. We present here three plans so that their virtues, defects, coverage, and costs can be compared. The plans differ in terms of how many families would receive help, the extent of the help they would receive, the quality of the care that each plan would offer, and, of course, what each plan would cost.

Plan 1—Fully Fund the Current Programs

A relatively modest interim plan would provide the resources to subsidize all families who are currently eligible for help under the programs that already exist in each state. These programs, largely financed by the federally funded Child Care and Development Fund (CCDF), now give benefits to only 10–15 percent of those who are eligible. Providing benefits to all income-eligible families nationally *who currently have their children in paid care*, and allotting child care subsidies as well to 60 percent of welfare recipients, is estimated to cost $19 billion a year.[16]

Reimbursements to providers would total $22 billion, of which $3 billion or 12 percent would be covered by parents' co-payments. The states might bear some of this cost, as they do under the present program, but presumably the federal government would continue to pay the lion's share. This program would give benefits to an estimated 9 million children, as compared with the 1–2 million currently estimated to be getting benefits under the federal block grants and associated state funds.[17]

The child care subsidy programs operating under the CCDF have major weaknesses in addition to the insufficient funding: 1) help is cut off abruptly as a family's income rises, leaving many families with moderate incomes without access to affordable care, as we have defined it, and 2) the reimbursement rates to providers that the programs allow are not based on quality considerations. The interim plan does not cure these two latter weaknesses. That is done by the second plan presented below.

Plan 2—Affordable Care of Improved Quality

A national plan that would be a worthy longer-term goal would allow all families, not just those with the lowest incomes, access to affordable care, as we have defined it. It would offer reimbursement rates to providers that would pay the cost of providing all children with care at a level of quality equal to the current national average. It would also incorporate a system of giving providers a bonus payment if they achieved higher quality. And as a family's income rises, the subsidies would be phased out gradually. The subsidy to which a family is entitled would not decrease by more than its increase in income, leaving the family worse off.[18]

What quality of care would this program finance? This would be determined by the amount providers would be allowed to charge, and by the licensing and inspection system that would oversee the eligible providers. Data from the study of Cost, Quality, and Child Outcomes in Child Care Centers (CQO) (Cost, Quality, and Child Outcomes Study Team 1995) allow us to relate the quality of the service provided to its cost. Using standard techniques, the study rated the quality of centers, giving scores from 1 to 7. Centers scoring 3 are designated in this system as "minimally adequate"; centers that use what child care professionals call "developmentally appropriate practices" are rated 5 and are given the designation "good." The average grade given centers in the study was 4. Average annual cost per child for centers rated 4, updated to prices charged in the year 2000, would be $7,380, and for those rated 5, $8,527.[19]

If we sent all child care providers a fee typical of providers giving care rated as "good," we would be paying for a standard that only a distinct minority of the nation's child care providers currently meet. Only

24 percent of the care provided to preschoolers by centers observed by the CQO study were given a rating of "good" or better. Centers providing care of that quality for infants and toddlers were even rarer: only 8 percent of the care they received in centers observed was rated "good" or better (Cost, Quality, and Child Outcomes Study Team 1995, pp. 26–27). The care in family day care homes and that given by friends and relatives is likely to be poorer still on average.

It would seem sensible to pay for the quality standard that the average provider currently meets (a grade of 4, which, of course, about half do not meet), which would entail paying centers $6,339 for preschool children and $10,865 for the care of infants. We have set the reimbursement for family child care at $5,300 and $8,550, respectively. In estimating the cost of the program, we have included funds to allow extra payments ($1,150 annually per child) to providers whose quality reaches the "good" level.[20] These extra funds would provide an incentive to improve care, and be available to finance better pay for child care workers.

Table 4 gives examples of the benefits this program would pay. For single parents with one infant using center care, subsidies would be available for those with incomes below $65,560. A single parent with an infant and a preschooler would be partially subsidized for incomes up to $99,153. The final example given is the married couple with a single child in elementary school, needing after-school and summer care. In this case, parents would not receive subsidies above an income of $22,020, because above that income the fee is less than 20 percent of their over-the-poverty-line income.

To serve children currently needing care, plus those children of mothers expected to transit from welfare to work under this plan would, I estimate, cost $37 billion per year. If one-third of the children not currently in paid care had to be taken care of in addition, the cost of this plan would rise to $49 billion per year; the entry of two-thirds into paid care would require $61 billion. These figures include the cost of the quality bonus. Under current conditions, that would amount to 3 percent of expenditures under the program. However, if providers responded by upgrading their program quality, as would be hoped, that cost would grow.

Table 4 Illustrative Plan to Provide "Affordable Care of Improved Quality" at a 20% Co-Payment Rate

Parent(s)/child's age	Single/1		Single/1,4		Married/1		Married/10	
Cost of care ($)	10,865		17,204		10,865		1,780	
Poverty line ($)	11,235		13,133		13,120		13,120	
Wage ($)	Gov't pays	Parent pays	Gov't pays	Parent pays	Gov't pays	Parent pays	Gov't pays	Parent pays
10,000	10,865	0	17,204	0	10,865	0	1,780	0
12,000	10,712	153	17,204	0	10,865	0	1,780	0
14,000	10,312	553	17,031	173	10,689	176	1,604	176
16,000	9,912	953	16,631	573	10,289	576	1,204	576
18,000	9,512	1,353	16,231	973	9,889	976	804	976
20,000	9,112	1,753	15,831	1,373	9,489	1,376	404	1,376
22,000	8,712	2,153	15,431	1,773	9,089	1,776	4	1,776
24,000	8,312	2,553	15,031	2,173	8,689	2,176	0	1,780
26,000	7,912	2,953	14,631	2,573	8,289	2,576	0	1,780
28,000	7,512	3,353	14,231	2,973	7,889	2,976	0	1,780
30,000	7,112	3,753	13,831	3,373	7,489	3,376	0	1,780
32,000	6,712	4,153	13,431	3,773	7,089	3,776	0	1,780
34,000	6,312	4,553	13,031	4,173	6,689	4,176	0	1,780
36,000	5,912	4,953	12,631	4,573	6,289	4,576	0	1,780
38,000	5,512	5,353	12,231	4,973	5,889	4,976	0	1,780
40,000	5,112	5,753	11,831	5,373	5,489	5,376	0	1,780

42,000	4,712	6,153	11,431	5,773	5,089	5,776	0	1,780
44,000	4,312	6,553	11,031	6,173	4,689	6,176	0	1,780
46,000	3,912	6,953	10,631	6,573	4,289	6,576	0	1,780
48,000	3,512	7,353	10,231	6,973	3,889	6,976	0	1,780
50,000	3,112	7,753	9,831	7,373	3,489	7,376	0	1,780
52,000	2,712	8,153	9,431	7,773	3,089	7,776	0	1,780
54,000	2,312	8,553	9,031	8,173	2,689	8,176	0	1,780
56,000	1,912	8,953	8,631	8,573	2,289	8,576	0	1,780
58,000	1,512	9,353	8,231	8,973	1,889	8,976	0	1,780
60,000	1,112	9,753	7,831	9,373	1,489	9,376	0	1,780
62,000	712	10,153	7,431	9,773	1,089	9,776	0	1,780
64,000	312	10,553	7,031	10,173	689	10,176	0	1,780
66,000	0	10,865	6,631	10,573	289	10,576	0	1,780
68,000	0	10,865	6,231	10,973	0	10,865	0	1,780
70,000	0	10,865	5,831	11,373	0	10,865	0	1,780
72,000	0	10,865	5,431	11,773	0	10,865	0	1,780
74,000	0	10,865	5,031	12,173	0	10,865	0	1,780
76,000	0	10,865	4,631	12,573	0	10,865	0	1,780
78,000	0	10,865	4,231	12,973	0	10,865	0	1,780
80,000	0	10,865	3,831	13,373	0	10,865	0	1,780
82,000	0	10,865	3,431	13,773	0	10,865	0	1,780

(continued)

66

Table 4 (continued)

Parent(s)/child's age	Single/1		Single/1,4		Married/1		Married/10	
Cost of care ($)	10,865		17,204		10,865		1,780	
Poverty line ($)	11,235		13,133		13,120		13,120	
Wage ($)	Gov't pays	Parent pays	Gov't pays	Parent pays	Gov't pays	Parent pays	Gov't pays	Parent pays
84,000	0	10,865	3,031	14,173	0	10,865	0	1,780
86,000	0	10,865	2,631	14,573	0	10,865	0	1,780
88,000	0	10,865	2,231	14,973	0	10,865	0	1,780
90,000	0	10,865	1,831	15,373	0	10,865	0	1,780
92,000	0	10,865	1,431	15,773	0	10,865	0	1,780
94,000	0	10,865	1,031	16,173	0	10,865	0	1,780
96,000	0	10,865	631	16,573	0	10,865	0	1,780
98,000	0	10,865	231	16,973	0	10,865	0	1,780

Plan 3—Free Universal Care

Finally, a plan that would provide free care to all families, regardless of income, on the basis of the same fee structure as the plan to provide affordable care of improved quality, but with zero co-payments, would cost $79–$129 billion per year. Were such a plan to be instituted, costs would quickly reach the top of that range and soon exceed it, as most parents would use it.

Child Care Versus Other National Needs

An adequate child care program is certainly not the only desirable public program lacking in the United States. The country lacks universal access to health care, including care for mental health; adequate funding for public schools, especially in low-income areas; access to higher education for anyone who can profit from it; immediate help for those addicted to drugs or alcohol; affordable housing; adequate public transportation; and adequate social services to counter child abuse, homelessness, and other social pathologies. To create such programs or to bring the ones we have to adequacy would require major expenditures of public money. The program we have outlined to provide the United States with affordable child care of improved quality would also, as we have seen, entail major new public expenditures, year after year. How high is the priority of such a child care program? Does it belong in the list of major national needs?

The strongest case for programs of child care subsidies such as those proposed above rests on the fact that they will prevent considerable misery to children and their families. Making child care of decent quality affordable to all families would result in safer, more educational, and more enjoyable care for children, and it would give a financial boost to severly low-income families in a nonstigmatizing way. If it had no other benefits, a program providing affordable child care would be amply justified by the fact that it is an indispensable part of the cure for child poverty, which afflicts almost one in five children in the United States. It would reduce enrollment in welfare-type programs, and it would give parents a chance to participate in the world of work and achieve the gains in resources and status that such a participation allows.

We do not really have to decide whether the benefits of the child care program are greater or less than the benefits from universal access to health care or the other desirable programs that are missing in the United States. Other countries can afford all these programs by requiring higher taxes and running a lower defense budget. The simple truth is that, like them, we can afford them all.

Notes

Financial support for this study was received from the Foundation for Child Development.

1. A U.S. Census survey in 1993 (Casper 1995) reported that those families with monthly incomes less than $1,200 spent on average 25 percent of their incomes on child care while the mother worked.
2. The other causes cited by Representative Tom DeLay, Republican Whip, were the teaching of evolution and the smallness of families due to working women's use of contraceptives (Noonan 1999, p. 16).
3. The U.S. Census Bureau reports payments for 1993 (Casper 1995), and these figures have been annualized for full-time service and adjusted to the year 2000 by use of the child care component of the Consumer Price Index.
4. See http://www.bls.gov
5. Single mothers paid for 46.6 percent of child care arrangements (Casper 1995). However, many families had more than one arrangement. A mother of two might have one paid arrangement and one unpaid one.
6. The National Academy of Science method of explicit budgeting also allows one to take account of regional differences in housing costs (Citro and Michael 1995). See also Renwick and Bergmann (1993).
7. The National Academy of Science experts did not propose a standard child care cost, as was done for other types of family expenditures. In deciding whether to count a family as poor, they subtracted a family's actual child care costs from its disposable income before comparing its resources to the basic budget. This decision can be criticized on the ground that some of the free or low-cost care arrangements that families make because they have no alternative are seriously substandard.
8. The data collected by the "Cost, Quality, and Outcomes" study permits an estimate of the costs associated on average with each level of quality. These reported costs were updated to the year 2000 using the child care component of the Consumer Price Index. The average quality of care currently given in centers is better than "minimally adequate," but it does not reach the standard the experts have rated "good" or "developmentally appropriate."

9. We are assuming she receives health insurance from her employer. If she doesn't she would need a still higher wage income, because the poverty line includes nothing for health care.

10. At that wage she would no longer be eligible to benefit from the EITC or food stamps, and she would have to pay $2,598 in Social Security taxes. She would benefit from the recently enacted $500 per child federal tax credit and the tax for dependent care expenses. She would end up paying $1,103 in federal income tax. In most states, she would have to pay a state income tax; in Colorado, the state we are using as an example, it would amount to $364.

11. Computed by the author from wages reported by single mothers in the 1999 Current Population Survey, which refers to incomes for the year 1998. The wages quoted were converted into dollars of the year 2000.

12. This condition is violated by current state plans. Under the federal rules which govern it, an increase of income of a few dollars can reduce the subsidy by thousands of dollars.

13. In theory, a phaseout rate of 100 percent would be possible. However, losing a dollar in child care benefit for every dollar gained in pre-tax income would leave the family worse off the more income it earned. It would have to pay tax on each dollar of new income, so it would lose $1 of benefit but gain less than a dollar in spending power. In practice, 50 percent is close to the fastest rate of phaseout of the child care benefit for the lower income groups that would allow them, when their wage income rises, to have more income left over after paying for child care rather than less. The reason is that as their income rises, their benefits from the EITC and food stamps are being reduced and the Social Security tax has to be paid.

14. This kind of counterproposal was made, for example, by President George Bush who, when the Congress then controlled by the Democratic party, made child care subsidy proposals during his administration.

15. Undoubtedly, some unlicensed care is of high quality. If some forms of care, such as relative care, cannot be licensed or are unlikely to be licensed, then there will be cases where giving a subsidy causes a child to be shifted from higher- to lower-quality care. However, most studies suggest that licensed care is on average superior to unlicensed care, relative care included.

16. These estimates do not take into account large differences in child care costs from one area to another within the United States. Some are due to differences in average quality and in the cost of living. Such differences would considerably complicate the design of a national program.

17. Estimated by the author on the basis of Congressional estimates that about 1 million families are covered by various child care programs, as of 1997 (U.S. House of Representatives, Committee on Ways and Means 1999).

18. This condition is violated by current state plans under the CCDF. Under the federal rules which govern it, an increase of income of a few dollars can reduce the subsidy by thousands of dollars.

19. These figures were derived from the data generated by the CQO study, increased by the change in child care prices, as measured by the child care index of the Consumer Price Index, between mid 1992 and February 2000.
20. This amount is the estimated difference in costs between centers graded 4 and 5 by the "Cost, Quality, and Outcomes Study," taking into account 1998 child care prices.

References

Bergmann, Barbara R. 1996. *Saving Our Children From Poverty: What the United States Can Learn From France*. New York: Russell Sage Foundation.

Casper, Lynne M. 1995. "What Does It Cost to Mind Our Preschoolers?" *Current Population Reports*, P70-52. U.S. Bureau of the Census, Washington, D.C., September.

Citro, Constance F., and Robert T. Michael. 1995. *Measuring Poverty: A New Approach*. Washington, D.C.: National Academy Press.

Cost, Quality, and Child Outcomes Study Team. 1995. *Cost, Quality, and Child Outcomes in Child Care Centers, Public Report*. Economics Department, University of Colorado at Denver.

Kaus, Mickey. 1992. *The End of Equality*. New York: Basic Books.

Noonan, David. 1999. "Seven Days: The Last Word on Last Week." *New York Daily News*, June 20, p. 16.

Peritz, Ingrid. 2000. "Tired of the Kids? Try 24-Hour Day Care; Quebec Tests Program Aimed at Shift Workers." *The Globe and Mail*, August 31.

Presser, Harriet B. 1989. "Some Economic Complexities of Child Care Provided by Grandmothers." *Journal of Marriage and the Family* 51(August): 581–591.

Renwick, Trudi J., and Barbara R. Bergmann. 1993. "A Budget-Based Definition of Poverty, With an Application to Single-Parent Families." *Journal of Human Resources* 28(1): 1–24.

U.S. Bureau of Labor Statistics. 2000. "Families with Own Children: Employment Status of Parents by Age of Youngest Child and Family Type, 1998–99 Annual Average," http://stats.bls.gov/news.release/famee.t04.htm.

U.S. House of Representatives, Committee on Ways and Means. 1999. *The 1998 Green Book*. Washington, D.C.: Government Printing Office.

3

Parents' Work Time and the Family

Thirty Years of Change

Cordelia W. Reimers
*Hunter College and the Graduate School
of the City University of New York*

The last three decades of the twentieth century have been a time of enormous change for U.S. families—change in family size and structure, in time parents worked for pay, in income and who earned it, and in how child rearing and other household tasks are managed. More children are living with only one parent, and their mothers are working a greater number of hours outside the home. Median family income has stagnated, but inequality has increased. At the same time, families are having fewer children. Some of these changes have contributed to lower incomes and limited parental time available to children; others have done the opposite.

This chapter will discuss five broad trends since 1969 that have affected families with children: 1) changes in family structure with the rise of single-parent families, 2) changes in parents' paid work time as mothers worked more outside the home, 3) change (or rather, lack thereof) in median family income, 4) changes in the distribution of income among families as inequality grew, and 5) changes in the number of children per family as families became smaller. The chapter will survey these trends, discuss some of the underlying reasons behind them, and examine how families with children are faring in the face of all these changes. It concludes with a description of the challenges facing policymakers at the turn of the century.

The data are drawn from the Current Population Survey (CPS) microdata files for March 1970, 1980, 1990, 1997, and 2000.[1] These surveys contain information about annual income from various sources in the previous year, as well as weeks and usual hours worked and a variety of demographic characteristics.[2] They include a random sam-

ple of about 50,000 households representing the noninstitutionalized
population in the United States. Hispanic-headed households are over-
sampled. When families are selected that have children under age 18
and whose head is a civilian at least 18 years old, 21,287 families are in
our sample in 1970 and 18,619 in 2000.[3] We tabulate labor force participation, hours and weeks worked, earnings, and income from other
sources for families classified by a few demographic variables: gender,
marital status, education, and race or Hispanic ethnicity of the family
head; and age of the youngest child. All incomes are expressed in constant 1999 dollars.[4] We also draw on published tabulations from the
CPS describing the labor force participation of mothers of infants
under one year old (Bachu and O'Connell 2000).

INCREASE IN SINGLE-PARENT FAMILIES

One of the most important changes in the last 30 years has been the
tremendous expansion of the share of families with children that have
only one parent in the home. Due to more divorce and out-of-wedlock
childbearing, this share climbed from 13 percent in 1969 to 30 percent
in 1999.[5] Half of this increase occurred in the 1970s alone, and the
expansion of the share of families with single parents has been deceler-
ating since. Still, the number of one-parent families has continued to
grow faster than the number with two parents, so the fraction of families that have only one parent present continues to rise. Single parents
have only half as much total time as two parents, and typically have
less than half as much earning power. The rising number of single parents has therefore increased the fraction of families that are strapped
for both cash and time for child care.

INCREASED PAID WORK TIME BY MOTHERS

Another dramatic change in the past 30 years has been the huge
shift of mothers out of the household and into the labor market. The
total hours parents work at paid jobs have increased enormously since

1969, by 540 hours per year, or 19 percent, for married couples (Figure 1), and by 441 hours, or 42 percent, for single parents. This is entirely because of the increasing amount of time mothers are devoting to earning money. Single parents are mostly (but not all) women. Married fathers' paid work time has declined slightly, as they worked the equivalent of one week less in 1999 than in 1969, on average. The drop occurred in the 1970s, as married fathers' annual hours of work dropped by 100 hours in that decade. They remained constant in the 1980s and then rose by 46 hours in the 1990s. In contrast, married mothers' paid work time nearly doubled between 1969 and 1999, as they worked almost 600 hours, or 96 percent more.

All dimensions of mothers' paid work time have risen: more mothers have paid jobs, they are employed more weeks in a year, and they are working more hours each week. As married mothers entered the workforce in unprecedented numbers, their employment rate rose from 36 percent during the survey week in 1970 to 65 percent in 2000 (Figure 2). They caught up with single parents in 1990, but then single parents pulled ahead again as they moved into the workforce in large numbers in the 1990s. Overall, the single parents' employment rate rose from 53 percent in 1970 to 71 percent in 2000. Moreover, married mothers who were in the labor force worked an average of 45 weeks in 1999, the same as single parents. This is an increase of six weeks since 1969 for the married women, and almost two weeks for the single parents. Average weekly hours also increased, by two and one-quarter hours for married mothers and by half as much for single parents. Nevertheless, in 2000 married mothers still spent fewer hours per week at paid jobs (35.2) than single parents did (38.8).

These increases occurred at different times for married and single mothers. The big increases for married mothers were in the 1970s and 1980s. Their annual hours of paid employment rose only half as much in the 1990s as in the previous decade (see Figure 1). In contrast, time worked by single parents surged between 1996 and 1999, after the enactment of welfare reform. As a result, their annual hours increased more in the 1990s than in the previous two decades combined. The labor force participation rate of never-married mothers aged 15–44 rose from 57 percent to 60 percent between 1990 and 1995, and then jumped to 68 percent in 1998 (Figure 3). In contrast, the labor force participation rate of never-married women in this age group *without*

Figure 1 Total Annual Hours of Paid Work, Married Couples with Children under 18

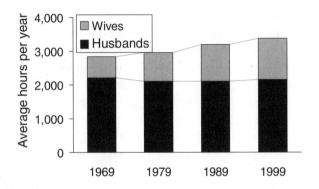

SOURCE: March CPS microdata files.

Figure 2 Employment Rates for Parents with Children under 18

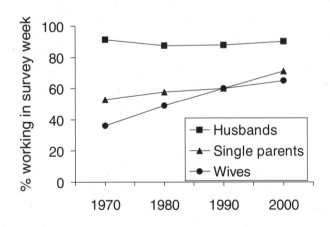

SOURCE: March CPS microdata files.

Figure 3 LFPR of Never-Married Women Age 15–44

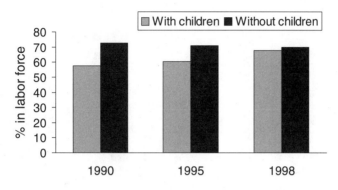

SOURCE: March CPS microdata files.

children slipped from 72 percent to 70 percent between 1990 and 1998. This suggests that welfare reform, not simply the tightening labor market, was behind the surge of single parents into the workforce in the 1990s.

The increase in mothers' work for pay has not been uniform; rather, it differs between more- and less-educated women, by race/ethnicity, and between those with and without young children in the home. The greatest increases have been for the married women with the most education. College-educated married mothers doubled their annual hours of paid work in the last 30 years of the twentieth century, from 677 to 1,362 for those with a BA or more, and from 606 to 1,274 for those without a BA (Figure 4). Married mothers who did not go beyond high school increased their annual hours of paid work by 75 percent, from 618 to 1,083. Among single parents, on the other hand, paid work time rose less for those with college degrees than for the less educated, who worked fewer annual hours to start with. Single parents with a BA or more went from working 1,604 hours in 1969 to 1,871 in 1999, an increase of 17 percent. Those with some college went from 1,266 hours to 1,686, an increase of 33 percent, and those with no more than high school went from 1,004 hours to 1,319, an increase of 31 percent. The time patterns of these increases reflect the effects of welfare reform. The biggest increases for single parents with college educa-

Figure 4 Annual Hours Worked, by Education

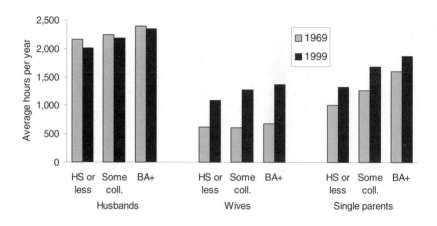

SOURCE: March CPS microdata files.

tions, as for married mothers at all education levels, were in the 1970s and 1980s; whereas the biggest increases for single parents with no more than high school were in the late 1990s.

Black and white non-Hispanic married mothers' paid work time increased by about 400 hours, almost twice as much as Hispanics', between 1979 and 1999 (Figure 5).[6] Because the white women started from a lower base, their percentage increase was greater than the blacks': 50 percent versus 37 percent. The Hispanic wives' increase of 222 hours per year was a rise of 28 percent. Among single parents, however, the race/ethnic pattern is just the reverse. Hispanics had the largest, and white non-Hispanics the smallest, increases in annual hours of paid work, in both numerical and percentage terms. Hispanic single parents' paid employment climbed by 423 hours, or 48 percent; blacks' climbed by 412 hours, or 43 percent; and white non-Hispanics' rose by 284 hours, or 21 percent.

The largest increases have been among mothers of very young children, who had the lowest rates of market work to begin with. Both

Figure 5 Annual Hours Worked, by Race/Ethnicity

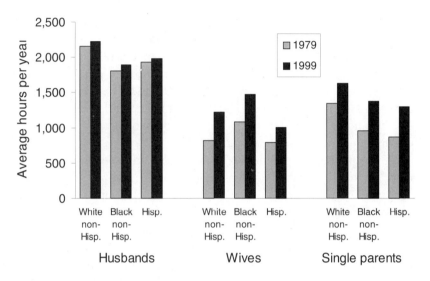

SOURCE: March CPS microdata files.

Figure 6 Annual Hours Worked, by Age of Youngest Child

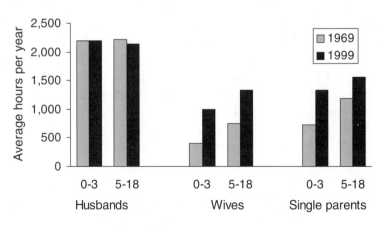

SOURCE: March CPS microdata files.

single parents and married mothers with children below age three increased their paid work time by 600 hours, on average, between 1969 and 1999 (Figure 6). For the single parents, this represented an increase of 82 percent. For the married mothers it was an increase of two and a half *times*. By 1999 married mothers with children under three years old were working outside the home 1,000 hours a year, which is equivalent to a half-time job. (A full-time job—40 hours a week for 50 weeks a year—would be 2,000 hours.) Their husbands' annual hours did not change. As a result, total parental work time outside the home increased by 23 percent for two-parent families with children under three years of age.

Even mothers of infants under one year old have surged into the labor force. Their labor force participation rate climbed from 31 percent in 1976 to 59 percent in 1998 (Bachu and O'Connell 2000). The rate of increase slowed somewhat after 1986, when their labor force participation rate reached 50 percent; but it jumped again by 3.7 percentage points from 1995 to 1998.

The effects of welfare reform are evident in the greater increases in labor force participation after 1995 by never-married and minority mothers and those with less education. The labor force participation rate of never-married women with infants climbed from 40 to 47 percent in the first half of the 1990s, and then to 54 percent in the next three years (Figure 7). Married mothers of infants are still more likely to be in the paid workforce, however. In 1998 their participation rate was 60 percent.

For black women with infants, married or not, participation in the workforce rose from 47 percent in 1990 to 52 percent in 1995, and then jumped by 11 points to 63 percent in 1998, putting them well ahead of whites as well as Hispanics (Figure 8). For Hispanic mothers of infants, labor force participation had dropped from 44 percent to 39 percent in the first half of the 1990s; then it bounced back to 46 percent in the next three years. The increases were larger at the lower education levels; but still, in 1998 mothers of infants who had a BA degree or more were much more likely to be in the workforce than those with no more than a high school diploma: 68 percent versus 38 percent (Figure 9).

The increases in annual hours of paid work for mothers whose children were all of school age were somewhat less dramatic than for those with younger children, but were nonetheless quite large: 374 hours (31

Figure 7 LFPR of Mothers Aged 15–44 Who Had a Child in the Last Year, by Marital Status

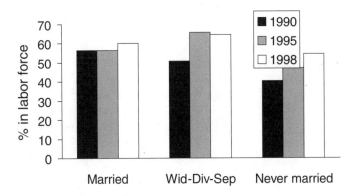

SOURCE: Bachu and O'Connell 2000.

Figure 8 LFPR of Mothers Aged 15–44 Who Had a Child in the Last Year, by Race/Ethnicity

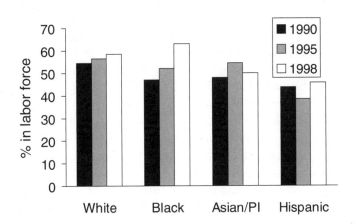

SOURCE: Bachu and O'Connell 2000.

Figure 9 LFPR of Mothers Aged 15–44 Who Had a Child in the Last Year, by Education

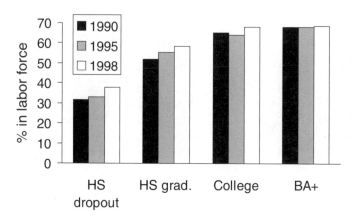

SOURCE: Bachu and O'Connell 2000.

percent) for single parents and 577 hours (77 percent) for the married women (see Figure 6). The fathers' annual hours declined very slightly (82 hours, or 4 percent), so total parental time in the labor market increased by 17 percent for two-parent families with only school-aged children.

What is behind this dramatic shift of mothers from the home to the workplace? A fundamental force has been rising wages for women. Women's median full-time year-round real earnings (in 1999 dollars) climbed from $21,045 in 1969 to $26,324 in 1999, a rise of 25 percent (U.S. Census Bureau 2001a). This has made time spent in unpaid activities at home and elsewhere increasingly costly to the family, in terms of foregone income. A mother who stays home today is making a bigger sacrifice of income than ever before.

The stagnation of men's median wages during much of this period, with declining wages for low-skilled male workers, has reinforced this pressure. In 1969 the median man who worked full time all year earned $35,751 in 1999 dollars; in 1999 he earned $36,476, just 2 percent more (U.S. Census Bureau 2001a). In the interim, men's median full-time year-round real earnings had fluctuated with the business cycle but with a downward trend, peaking in 1973 at $39,483, in 1978 at $38,824, and in 1986 at $38,391. With fathers already working full time for the most part, the only way for most families to increase their income—and for many simply to maintain it in the face of falling male wages—has been for the woman to take a job or work more hours. The narrowing gender wage gap, as women's full-time earnings rose from 58.9 to 72.2 percent of men's, has created powerful pressure toward a more equal division of labor within the family, with mothers and fathers sharing both financial responsibilities and household tasks, rather than specializing with a male breadwinner and female full-time homemaker.

However, the magnitudes of the changes in women's paid work time are still not completely understood, and they are not easily explained by changes in key economic variables (Blau 1998; Danziger and Reed 1997). The increases in paid work among women seem to be more closely related to increases in their own wages than to the changes in their husband's wages over this period (Juhn and Murphy 1997). Diminished discrimination against women in the workplace and removal of barriers that had kept them out of nontraditional occupations have also encouraged women to expand their work outside the home. Highly educated women have benefited more from diminished discrimination than have women with less education, as higher-level professional and management jobs have opened up to them.

Finally, attitudes toward working mothers have changed, making it the norm rather than the exception for a woman to have a paid job, even while her children are toddlers. This change in attitudes is, of course, not unrelated to the pressures from rising wages for women and the narrowing gender wage gap discussed above. A self-reinforcing set of reciprocal influences is operating here, in which rising wages induce more mothers to go to work, which in turn makes it a more "normal" pattern, which in turn reduces the social pressure to stay at home while children are young. Furthermore, as women have more continuous careers with less time out for childrearing, their accumulated work experience increases and with it, their rate of wage growth over time. This in turn encourages more women to train for and pursue highly paid careers.

NO GROWTH IN MEDIAN FAMILY INCOME—UNTIL THE LAST FEW YEARS

Putting the trends in wages and hours together, to what extent have increases in hours of paid work within families translated into increases in family income? When all families are lumped together, the median family's pre-tax cash income rose just 12 percent (from $42,039 to $47,100) in the last three decades of the twentieth century, after adjusting for inflation. Virtually all of this gain occurred in the last three years, as median income had risen only 1.5 percent between 1969 and 1996. It then jumped 10 percent in the next three years. Because families in the upper tail gained the most (and gained much more than those in the lower tail lost), average real family income rose 27 percent (from $46,447 to $58,888 in 1999 dollars) over the 30-year period—14 percent in the 27 years from 1969 to 1996 and another 11 percent in the three years from 1996 to 1999.[7]

The modest overall rise in family income is the outcome of four offsetting trends: rising earnings for women, stagnating male wages, declining real value of transfer payments, and the shift toward single parenthood. Largely because of women's increasing work time and wages, average family incomes for both married-couple and single-parent families rose (by 44 percent and 26 percent, respectively), even though fathers' earnings stagnated during most of the period, and real transfer income for single parents fell. But at the same time an increasing share of families were headed by single parents, whose incomes are much lower than those of families with two earners. This shift cancelled the extra gains for married-couple families taken separately, leaving overall average family income only 27 percent higher—and median family income only 12 percent higher—after thirty years.[8]

Figures 10 and 11 present estimates of average family incomes, by income component. Similar to the median family incomes discussed above, they measure pre-tax cash income only, including cash benefits such as welfare and unemployment insurance benefits, but they do not include other family resources, such as fringe benefits, food stamps, and the Earned Income Tax Credit (EITC). While these other resources and taxes are important, they are difficult to measure accurately or consistently for individual families. Because food stamp use

Figure 10   Average Family Income of Married Couples with Children under 18, by Source

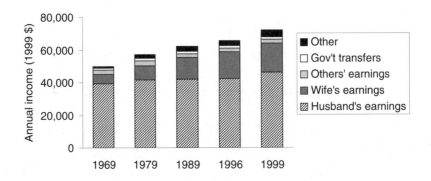

SOURCE: March CPS microdata files.

Figure 11   Average Family Income of Single Parents with Children under 18, by Source

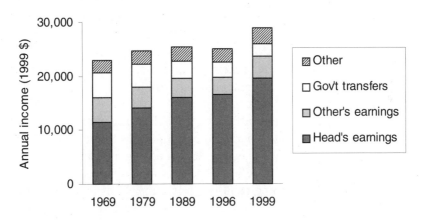

SOURCE: March CPS microdata files.

grew rapidly in the 1970s and the EITC expanded greatly in the 1990s, the pre-tax cash income measure omits more of the resources available to low-income families today than in the 1960s. The family income data therefore understate the gains made by low-income families since 1969.[9]

An analysis of the components of married parents' total family income shows that the wives' rising earnings were the main source of income growth. After rising only 6 percent in real terms between 1969 and 1996, fathers' wages rose by 10 percent in the next three years alone, resulting in an increase of 17 percent over the period 1969–1999. Meanwhile, their annual hours of paid work declined slightly, by 2.5 percent, between 1969 and 1999. The combination resulted in an 18 percent increase in fathers' annual earnings, more than half of it coming in 1996–1999 alone (see Figure 10).[10] In contrast, married mothers' wages increased by 57 percent and their annual hours of work for pay nearly doubled; therefore, their annual earnings more than tripled. Government transfers for two-parent families—such as Social Security and Supplemental Security Income for the disabled, unemployment insurance, veterans' benefits, and workers' compensation—rose by 22 percent, but they represent less than 2 percent of these families' income. Other sources of income—earnings of other family members and unearned income—rose by 67 percent for two-parent families, but these represent less than 10 percent of family income. Largely because of women's rising wages, the average annual income of couples rose by more than their annual work time. In 1999 married parents spent 19 percent more total hours working for pay than in 1969, but their income was 44 percent higher.

The picture was quite different for single parents (mostly, but not all, female). Their wages increased by 33 percent from 1969 to 1999. Their work time rose by 42 percent, far exceeding the increase for couples, and their earnings rose by 70 percent (see Figure 11). But their income rose by only 26 percent, much less than their increase in paid work time. This was because the inflation-adjusted transfer income of single-parent families dropped by 50 percent over the 30-year period, and their income from other sources rose by only 4 percent. Because nominal AFDC benefits were not increased to keep up with inflation, their real value declined throughout the period. Then in the 1990s welfare reform led to a steep decline in welfare caseloads, further reducing the transfer income of single parents. On average, their 42 percent greater paid-work effort more than offset the loss of welfare, but it increased their total income by only a quarter.

MORE INEQUALITY

Another outcome of the trends of the past 30 years is greater inequality among families. Not only has income inequality risen within each type of family, but single parents have less time *and* less money than two parents—and many more families are in this situation. Because the average income of two-parent families increased by 44 percent while that of one-parent families increased by only 26 percent, the gap between them expanded. In 1969, married couples with children had 2.2 times the income of single parents, on average. By 1999, the ratio was 2.5.

Income Gaps by Education

Inequality of family incomes increased on other dimensions as well. Less-educated fathers lost earning power, and they worked less and had lower annual earnings in 1999 than 30 years before. This situation just began to improve in the last few years. Less-educated single parents lost transfer income from welfare benefits, which more than offset the improvement in their earnings relative to single parents with college educations.

Fathers without a bachelor's degree earned less, on average, in 1999 than in 1969 (Figure 12). Those with no more than a high school diploma earned 10 percent less in real terms; those with some college education earned 3 percent less. That the drop was not greater is due to a turnaround between 1996 and 1999. In 1996 average earnings of fathers with no college were 14 percent lower than in 1969; then they grew by 5 percent in the next three years. Even this improvement, however, did not quite get them back to where they had been in 1989, much less 1969. Fathers with some college suffered an 8 percent decline in annual earnings from 1969 to 1996, followed by a 6 percent improvement by 1999. This put them just barely ahead of where they

Figure 12 Average Annual Earnings of Married Parents, by Education

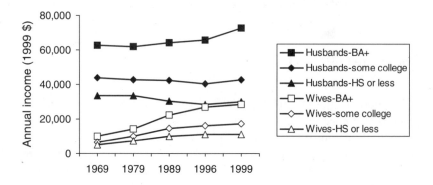

SOURCE: March CPS microdata files.

had been in 1989.   In contrast, fathers with a BA or more earned 16 percent more than they had in 1969. Their earnings rose just 5 percent from 1969 to 1996, but then climbed 10 percent in the next three years.

The wives did better. By dint of working many more hours and the rise in women's wages, married mothers at each education level earned two to three times as much in 1999 as 30 years earlier. Those with no more than a high school education earned 2.1 times as much, and those with college education earned 2.7–2.8 times as much (see Figure 12).

The faster earnings growth of more-educated fathers and mothers, combined with the tendency of more-educated men to marry more-educated women, caused the gap in total income between two-parent families with more- and less-educated heads to increase. Overall, the total income of married-couple families where the husband did not go beyond high school improved by just 15 percent in three decades, after adjusting for inflation (Figure 13). For families where the father had some college, total real income increased by 26 percent, and for those where he had at least a BA, the increase was 42 percent. As a result, the income gap between families with more- and less-educated heads expanded. In 1969, families whose head finished college had 1.7 times the income of families whose head did not go beyond high school. By 1999 this ratio was 2.1.

Figure 13 Average Family Income, by Marital Status and Education

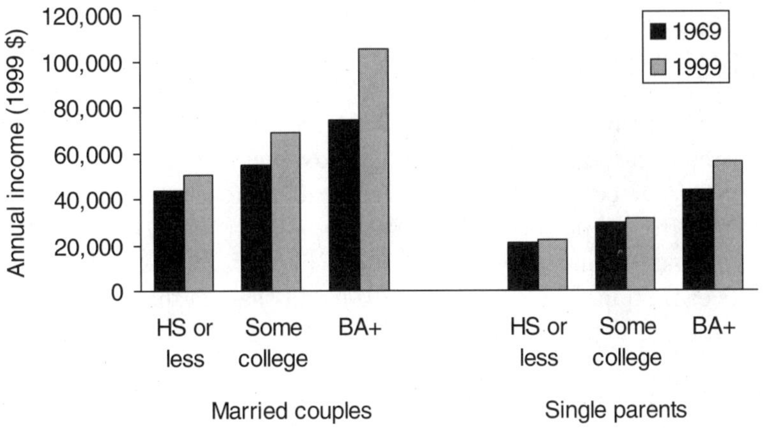

SOURCE: March CPS microdata files.

Among single parents, on the other hand, the earnings gap between the more- and less-educated narrowed, while the family income gap widened. Those with a high school education or less experienced a 39 percent rise in earnings from 1969 to 1999—17 percent in the 1970s, 3 percent in the 1980s, 1 percent from 1989 to 1996, and then a jump of 15 percent in the next three years. This no doubt reflects the effect of welfare reform, combined with the tight labor market for low-skilled labor so that parents leaving (or not going on) welfare could find jobs. In the early 1990s, the early welfare reforms under federal waivers apparently offset the recession for this lowest-skilled group of single parents. For single parents with some college (but not four years), earnings grew by 36 percent over the period 1969–1999. Again, the growth was concentrated in the 1970s and late 1990s: 23 percent in the 1970s, 1 percent in the 1980s, a *drop* of 7 percent in the early 1990s (no doubt reflecting the recession and slow recovery), and then a 17 percent rise in the late 1990s as the labor market tightened.

Single parents with a BA or higher gained 26 percent in earnings over 30 years. This was a smaller gain than for single parents with less education, but the college graduates had earned much more to begin with: more than three times as much as those with no more than a high school diploma, and almost twice as much as those with some college. The timing of the earnings growth for single parents with four or more years of college was different, too: a drop of 7 percent in the 1970s, a 26 percent gain in the 1980s, a 3 percent drop from 1989 to 1996, and an 11 percent increase during 1996–1999.

The outcome of the slower earnings growth for more educated single parents was to narrow the earnings advantage of those with at least four years of college over those with no more than a high school diploma, from a ratio of 3.3 in 1969 to 3.0 in 1999. However, their total income advantage *increased* from a ratio of 2.1 to 2.5 (see Figure 13), because transfer payments were a larger share of the income of the less-skilled, and their value was cut in half.

Income Gaps by Race/Ethnicity

Looking at married-couple and single-parent families separately, the family income gaps between blacks, Hispanics, and white non-Hispanics failed to narrow during the last three decades of the twentieth century. Indeed, among two-parent families, Hispanics fell further behind the other groups. The gaps between black and white non-Hispanic family incomes did not change for either type of family, nor did the gaps between Hispanic and other single-parent families.

Among married couples with children, white and black non-Hispanics' average family income both grew by 31 percent between 1979 and 1999, while Hispanics' family income grew by a mere 4 percent (see Figure 14).[11] All of the Hispanics' gain occurred in the last three years. Their real family income had deteriorated by 4 percent between 1979 and 1996, then gained 8 percent from 1996 to 1999. Among single parents, white and black non-Hispanics' average family income rose by 19 percent during the 20-year period, while that of Hispanics rose by 23 percent.

Therefore, the black/white gaps remained constant for each type of family, with black non-Hispanic two-parent families having 77 percent as much income as white non-Hispanics, and black non-Hispanic single-parent families having 68 percent as much income as their white counterparts. When both types of families are combined, however, blacks' average family income grew less than that of whites because of

Figure 14 Average Family Income, by Marital Status and Race/Ethnicity

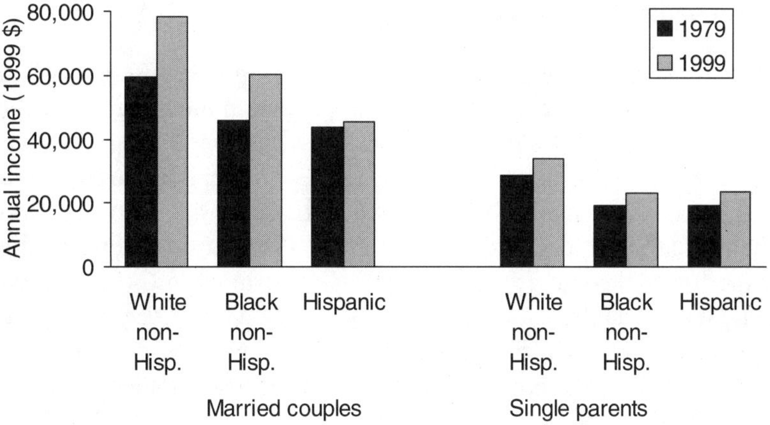

SOURCE: March CPS microdata files.

the larger share of single parents among blacks. Therefore, the overall black/white family income gap expanded.

Among one-parent families, the Hispanic/white gap was also virtually constant: Hispanics had 67 percent as much as white non-Hispanics in 1979, and 69 percent in 1999. There was little difference between Hispanic and black single parents' average family income in either year. But Hispanic two-parent families fell further behind blacks and whites over these two decades, slipping from 74 percent of white non-Hispanics' family incomes to only 58 percent. One reason was that Hispanic couples increased their combined paid work time much less than black and white non-Hispanic parents: 272 hours per year versus 479 and 475, respectively (see Figure 5). Another was that Hispanics' wages deteriorated relative to blacks' and whites' as the wage gap between more and less-skilled workers expanded, due to the Hispanics' lower average educational attainment (U.S. Census Bureau 2001b, 2001c, 2001d; McKinnon and Humes 2000; Therrien and Ramirez 2001). The increased immigration of Hispanics with very little education also contributed to the decline of their median wages (Schmidley and Gibson 1999).

Interquartile Income Gap

Putting together the various trends toward greater inequality, it is no surprise to find that families at the upper end of the income distribution gained while those in the lower tail lost out over the past 30 years. Families at the 75th percentile of all families with children experienced a 32 percent rise in real income, while those at the 25th percentile experienced an 11 percent decline. After 1996 the long-term decline for the lower income group reversed itself: from 1969 to 1996, total family income at the 25th percentile had dropped by 21 percent. It then rose by 12 percent in the next three years. The 75th percentile had risen by 19 percent from 1969 to 1996; then it rose another 11 percent in the next three years. As a result, between 1969 and 1996 families at the 75th percentile went from twice to more than triple the income of families at the 25th percentile, and the size of the gap did not change after that.

FEWER CHILDREN

At the same time that parents were working more outside the home and family incomes were increasing during the last three decades, the average number of children per family was decreasing, from 2.4 to 1.9. Declining fertility rates and later childbearing meant that, on average, there were 0.5 fewer children per family with children under 18 in 1989 than 1969. The number remained constant in the 1990s. The decline was somewhat greater in one-parent than two-parent families. In 1969 the average family with children under 18 had 2.4 children, regardless of whether there were two parents or one. Thirty years later the married couples had 1.9 children under 18 at home, whereas the single parents had only 1.7.

The same fundamental pressure—rising wages for women— underlies both the fertility decline and the dramatic shift of mothers' time into the labor market. The opportunity cost of child rearing, in terms of foregone income, has risen. And since the growth of female wages means that the cost of purchased child care rises about as fast as mothers' wages do, children simply have become much more expensive compared with other goods. Hence, parents are having fewer children.

NET OUTCOMES FOR CHILDREN

Family Per Capita Income

The combination of these dramatic trends since 1969—toward more parental time in the labor market and, consequently, more family income, but fewer children—means that there is more money per person for purchasing goods and services in many families, especially in those with two parents. But not all children have benefited. The increasing share of single-parent families, whose incomes are lower and grew much less than the incomes of married-couple families, needs to be taken into account. Moreover, less-skilled parents had slower income growth than highly skilled parents. It is therefore important to examine the trends in per capita income for lower-income and higher-income families, not just the average.

Figure 15 shows changes for the *combined* family income distribution of single-parent and two-parent families. As a crude adjustment for the differences in family size between two-parent and one-parent families and for the decreases in family size over time, family incomes are presented in per capita terms. (This adjustment overstates the gains from shrinking family size because it costs more than half as much to support one person as two.) The figure shows the change in average income per person for the lowest quarter, the highest quarter, and the middle half of the distribution of all families' per capita incomes, after adjusting for inflation.

These estimates indicate that while there has been substantial growth in real income per person for families with high per capita income, income per person was either stable or decreasing for other families when 1996 is compared with 1969. During the economic expansion from 1996 to 1999, however, families with lower per capita

**Figure 15 Average Income per Person, by Quartile, Families with
Children under 18**

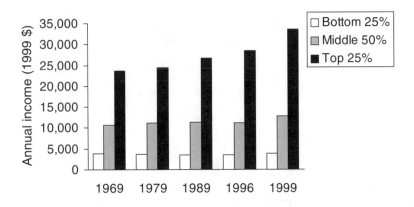

SOURCE: March CPS microdata files.

incomes also experienced rising income per person, though not as much as the high-income group. Between 1969 and 1999, the top quarter of families gained 42 percent ($9,877 in 1999 dollars), while families in the bottom quarter of the per capita income distribution had declines of three percent ($122), after adjusting for inflation. For families in the middle half of the per capita income distribution, average real income per person gained 20 percent ($2,098).

Potential Time for Children

The flip side of the increases in parents' paid work time and incomes is that parents have less time for other activities, thus less time potentially available for children. The information about what people actually do with the time they do not spend at paid jobs is limited, and comes mainly from time-use diary studies. These studies include only small samples of people. We begin with the CPS data regarding basic trends and then discuss the more detailed time-use diary data.

The CPS data indicate that families have less total time to devote to unpaid activities, including maintaining a household and caring for children, because they are spending more time in the labor market and because the share of families with a single parent is growing. From 1969 to 1999, both married-couple and single-parent families experienced a decrease in time not spent in paid work, of 1.4 hours and 1.2 hours, respectively. The overall decrease of 2.6 hours is greater than the decreases within either family type because the proportion of single-parent families increased over this period. It should be emphasized that this is a decrease only in time *potentially* available in the home. There is no information in the CPS about how parents actually spend their time outside paid work.

Despite increases in paid work hours for each type of family, reductions in family size mean that the amount of parental non-market time potentially available *per child* has increased for both married-couple and single-parent families since 1969. When single-parent and married-couple families are added together, however, the amount of parental time per child has remained relatively constant. This is because the shift toward more single parents tends to decrease total parental time available to children, as it reduces the number of custodial parents available to spend time with them. In any case, this measure is obviously misleading, because it assumes that an only child who spends an hour with a parent gets twice as much parental attention as each of two children who spend that same hour with the parent. This ignores the obvious "economies of scale" when a parent reads a story to, plays a game with, or eats a meal with more than one child at a time.

Time Use in the Home: Diary Evidence

The trends in hours of paid work time and non-market time described above are based on data that report individuals' estimates of their weeks worked and usual hours worked per week in the previous year. Such estimates may not accurately portray the actual hours worked for pay because the hours question is somewhat ambiguous and respondents may not be able to report accurately on a "usual" week in the few minutes allowed during the CPS interview. Fortunately, time-use diary surveys, which ask respondents to keep a detailed diary record of how they spend their time during a specific day, provide an alternative, more accurate method of measuring paid work time as well as time spent in various kinds of unpaid activities, such as commuting, housework, child care, shopping, recreation, and personal care. Time-use diary measures tend to show shorter paid work hours and sometimes even different trends than the CPS (Robinson and Godbey 1997, Chapter 5).

Unfortunately, such time-use diary surveys are conducted much less frequently and with much smaller samples than the CPS. The latest available data for adults were collected in 1985; results on parents' time use from a survey done in 1992–1994 are not yet available. More recent time-use diary data are available for children, however, as surveys were done in 1981 and 1997. Because of the small samples, time-use diary surveys cannot be used to examine trends for subgroups of the adult population, such as single parents or blacks. Moreover, the individuals who complete the diaries may not represent the U.S. population as well as the CPS sample does. These surveys do, however, provide otherwise unavailable information about how much time is spent by adults in different types of unpaid work at home, such as child care and housework, in leisure pursuits, and sleep. And the children's time-use diaries show recent trends in time children spend with their parents, in both married-couple and single-parent families. We first discuss the time-use diary evidence for parents, and then for children.

Time-use diaries for adults indicate that the entry of many mothers into the workforce has put them in a "time crunch." While both employed and non-employed women have managed to keep the amount of time spent with children relatively constant, a great many women with children have moved from the "non-employed" to "employed" category. The "time crunch" is best illustrated by the fact that in 1985, employed women spent more than one-third less time on child care and household tasks than women without paid jobs, but they still had 27 percent less free time (Robinson and Godbey 1997, Tables 3 and 6).

Figures 16 and 17 show the time devoted to various activities by all women and all men, including those without children, based on time-use surveys conducted in the United States in 1965 and 1985 (Robinson and Godbey 1997). The decreases in child care time for men and non-employed women reflect the fact that fewer of them are parents. The increase in child care time for employed women is mainly due to the shift of mothers into paid employment, which increased the share of the female workforce that had children at home. These same time-use surveys show that employed mothers spent almost the same

Figure 16 Women's Division of Time outside Paid Work and Sleep

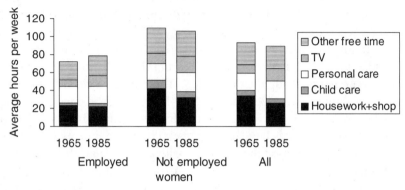

SOURCE: Robinson and Godbey 1997.

Figure 17 Men's Division of Time outside Paid Work and Sleep

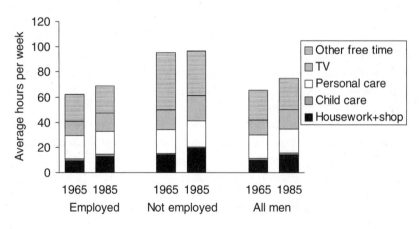

SOURCE: Robinson and Godbey 1997.

amount of time taking care of children in 1985 (6.7 hours per week) as in 1965 (6.3 hours per week).[12]   Mothers without paid jobs also maintained a consistent amount of time with children, spending about 12 hours a week on child care in both years.   When the shift of women into employment is taken into account, however, mothers' time in child care declined by 10 percent overall, from 10 to 9 hours per week. Fathers did not make up the difference. Their child care time remained about 2.6 hours per week from 1965 to 1985.   This suggests that the increase in market work among women has reduced parents' total child care time.   But mothers have reduced their child care time by much less than they have increased their time in paid work because they have cut back on other activities. Women have markedly reduced the time they spend on household chores.   Men have somewhat increased the time they spend on housework, but it does not make up for all of the reduction by women.

The effect of women's increased hours in the labor market on families is likely to vary between college-educated parents whose incomes have been rising faster than their work hours because their wages increased, and less-educated parents whose incomes have risen less than their work hours due to falling wages and transfer payments. The effect of women's increased paid work time on families is also likely to vary between married couples, who can shift some housework and child care from working wife to husband, and single parents, who cannot.   Within married-couple families, moreover, there are likely to be differences across education levels in this shifting of tasks, as child care time by fathers rises with their education.   Unfortunately, the time-use diary survey samples are too small to be broken down into these subsamples. Thus, the above-quoted estimates are based on average trends and may miss important distinctions between high- and low-income groups, or between single-parent and two-parent families.

Children's Time with Parents

The evidence we have from studies of time use in the home suggests that most of the extra paid work time by women has come out of household chores, not child care. The estimated reduction of time spent in child care is much less than the reduction in available time at home. When we also take into account the decrease in number of children per family, it is not at all clear that the average child today actually gets less time from a parent than 30 years ago.

Direct evidence from time-use diaries for children shows that in 1997 the average child spent more time with his or her parents than in 1981 (Sandberg and Hofferth 2001). This was true whether or not the mother was married, whether or not she worked, and whether or not she was a college graduate. This shift in parents' behavior far outweighed the negative effects of the increase in single parenthood and in mothers' paid employment. The net outcome was an increase of 4.3 hours per week (18 percent) spent with mothers and 3.0 hours per week (19 percent) spent with fathers. Because college-educated parents spend more time with a child than less-educated parents do, the rise in educational attainment helped, but it explains only a small part of the increase in children's time with their mothers.

Unfortunately, there are no data on children's time use before 1981, so we do not know what happened in the 1970s. It is possible that parental behavior adjusted with a lag, and that children's time with their parents declined in the 1970s as single parenthood and mothers' labor force participation grew. Therefore, we cannot say that children today spend more time with their parents than children did 30 years ago. However, several other considerations are relevant here. First, much of mothers' additional paid work time is at part-time jobs, often during school hours. In addition, couples often work different shifts so one of them can be at home with the children. This may not be good for their own relationship, but the children do have a parent around more often.

Moreover, in the past, even "stay-at-home" middle- and upper-class mothers, who didn't work for pay, were not at home with their children *all* the time. They went shopping, participated in church or synagogue groups, attended PTA and other organization meetings, did volunteer work in the community, played golf or bridge, and socialized. And even when their mothers were at home, school-aged children were often somewhere else—at school, at lessons, playing at friends' homes, or with baby-sitters.

As couples have shifted to a more equal division of labor from the traditional one where the father specialized in earning money and the mother in unpaid work in the household, the increase in mothers' earnings and the narrowing of the earnings gap between them and their husbands has given women more power within the family. This has both a down side and an up side for children. It may result in more divorced parents, because women today have more alternatives to staying in an unhappy marriage. But children may not be worse off living with only one parent than with an unhappy, perhaps violent, mother and father. And if parents do divorce or the father dies, the average mother today is better able to support the children alone than when she had no marketable skills. There is also some evidence that when the mother has more power within the family, the children benefit directly, as mothers are more likely than fathers to spend extra money on goods and services for children rather than on themselves.

SUMMARY AND CONCLUSIONS

This chapter has documented the large-scale shift of women's time from the home to the labor market over the last generation. For most families, this change has led to an increase in family income. It has also changed how child care and household tasks are done, with more purchased goods and fathers' time, but less total parental time because of less mothers' time. Take-out and pre-prepared convenience food, commercial laundries, landscapers, and housecleaning services consume much of the extra income parents earn. Child care is increasingly purchased from day care centers, nursery schools, baby-sitters, or nannies, depending on the parents' income level.

This chapter has also documented the very large shift from married-couple to single-parent families over the last 30 years, reducing both the income and parental time available for many children. While smaller family sizes have helped cushion the decrease in "home" time, many parents find it difficult to balance jobs and children. Single parents face the most difficulties. They have only half as much total time available as two parents, and a single mother typically has less than half as much earning power as a married couple because women's wages are lower than men's. Lack of income limits most single parents' ability to purchase time-saving goods and services and high-quality child care. Thus, they face a severe "time crunch" as well as a "money bind."

Among married parents, men without college educations have faced declining wages. While increased work by their wives has helped maintain their families' income, it is still difficult for these families to afford child care. Moreover, less-educated workers are less likely to have jobs that permit parents to arrange their hours to accommodate family needs.

Better-educated parents, whose increased time in the labor market has been rewarded with considerably higher incomes than in 1969, can more easily afford high-quality child care, household help, and other time-saving goods and services. Married-couple families, particularly those where the husband has a college degree, have seen substantial improvements in their economic situation over the last three decades. Even these couples, however, face the stress involved in balancing increased work and family.

If children and their families are going to withstand the stresses created by the trends of the last three decades, employers and public policy makers need to do more to help parents balance work and family. To an important extent, the effect of parents' market work time on children depends on when and where it is performed. By shifting from work in the home to work in the market, many women find themselves with far less flexibility in responding to family needs. Workplaces and work hours must become more flexible. Compensatory time instead of "time-and-a-half" pay for overtime work is one increasingly popular arrangement; "flextime" (that is, allowing employees some discretion in when they work their allotted hours) is another. In 1997, 28 percent of full-time wage and salary workers had flexible work schedules. This was up sharply from 15 percent in 1991, the most recent prior year when data were collected.[13] The Family and Medical Leave Act of 1993 enables workers to take up to 12 weeks of unpaid leave to care for a new baby or ailing family member without jeopardizing their jobs.

Flexibility in shift work enables parents to share child care more easily by working different shifts. In order for shift work to make combining paid work and child care easier, however, the choice of shifts must be voluntary. Nonstandard working hours may make it difficult both to find time to spend with children when they are awake and not in school and to arrange for child care while working. For those workers who cannot determine their own schedules, the combination of shift work and children is a potential source of stress and expense. In 1997,

83 percent of full-time wage and salary workers were on regular daytime schedules, 4.6 percent were on evening shifts, 3.9 percent were on employer-arranged irregular schedules, 3.5 percent were on night shifts, and 2.9 percent were on rotating shifts (Council of Economic Advisers 1999, p. 15).

Working at home for pay can also increase parents' flexibility. In 1997, 3.3 percent of all wage and salary workers were doing work at home for pay, up from 1.9 percent in 1991. An additional 10 percent of all wage and salary workers in 1997 were doing work at home without receiving extra pay for it. Nearly 9 out of 10 workers who were paid for work at home were in white-collar occupations (Council of Economic Advisers 1999, p. 15).

While incomes have been rising for most people, families at the bottom of the income distribution, whose inflation-adjusted incomes were lower in 1999 than in 1969, still face serious economic hardship. Many low-income parents are forced to work harder and spend less time with their families just to make ends meet. Policies that would help these families cope include expansions in the EITC; children's allowances or tax credits to help offset the expense of raising children; increases in the minimum wage; expanded child support enforcement; employer tax credits to help create jobs for welfare recipients; support for skill development among persons in lower-income families; and policies to encourage steady economic growth, which creates jobs, reduces unemployment, and raises wages for all workers—especially the less-skilled, who are most affected when jobs are scarce.

Since most parents adjust to an increase in their paid work time by increasing their use of child care providers, policies are also needed to help make child care more available and affordable and to improve its quality. The primary child care arrangements for preschool-aged children of employed mothers in the fall of 1994 were divided roughly equally among care in the child's home (by a relative or nonrelative), care in another home (by a relative or nonrelative), and care in an organized child care facility. Since comparable data were first collected in 1986, the trend shows a slight increase in the proportion of children receiving care in their own homes, relatively fewer children receiving care in another home, and relatively more children receiving care in an organized facility. In addition, the share of monthly income spent on child care by those purchasing this service rose from 6.3 percent to 7.3

percent between 1986 and 1993 (Council of Economic Advisers 1999, p. 16). More and higher-quality child care must be made available and affordable, with longer hours to accommodate parents who work irregular hours, and with after-school care for older children. The availability, cost, and quality of child care are crucial to the ability of parents to balance the needs of work and family and the well-being of their children.

Finally, policies that encourage economic expansion are extremely important, especially for less-skilled parents. It is not clear whether the earnings and income gains made by families with less-educated parents in 1996–1999 will persist in the long run, or whether they were a short-term phenomenon due to the extremely tight labor market during those years, combined with welfare reform.

Notes

I wish to thank the directors of the Werner Sichel Lecture-Seminar Series, Professor Emily P. Hoffman and Dr. Jean Kimmel, for their extraordinary hospitality. My lecture was based on the report *Families and the Labor Market, 1969–1999: Analyzing the "Time Crunch"* (Council of Economic Advisers, May 1999), which was written while I was a senior economist at the Council of Economic Advisers. I wish to thank Rebecca Blank, Maria Hanratty, Nora Gordon, Andrew Feldman, and others who also worked on that report. New data have been added to this chapter to update and expand the findings. All interpretations are my own.

1. Because the annual employment and income data collected each March refer to the previous calendar year, our data are for 1969, 1979, 1989, 1996, and 1999. Those years (with the exception of 1996) represent business-cycle peaks and thus trace out long-term trends. The year 1996 is included because the Personal Responsibility and Work Opportunity Reconciliation Act, or "welfare reform," was enacted in that year. This legislation had a profound effect on the labor supply of low-skilled single parents.

2. Annual hours of work in 1979, 1989, 1996, and 1999 were calculated by multiplying the answers to two questions which ask how many weeks each individual worked in the previous year and how many hours they "usually worked" in the weeks they worked. The 1969 data are not strictly comparable to later years due to differences in data reporting. An imputation procedure was used to make these data more comparable to information in later years.

3. The Census Bureau's definition of a *family* is used throughout this chapter; that is, all related individuals living together in the same household.   The analysis is restricted to families whose head is a civilian at least 18 years old and where there

is a child under age 18. A mother (or couple) and her (their) children living in a household headed by another family member are part of the head's family, and an unmarried parent cohabiting with a domestic partner is classified as a single parent. Throughout this chapter, unless otherwise specified, the terms *wives* and *married women* refer only to those with children.

4. The CPI-U-X1 price index is used to adjust for changes in prices over time. The CPI-U-X1 is an alternative to the CPI-U (Consumer Price Index for Urban Consumers) that uses the rental equivalence approach to improve the treatment of home ownership costs before 1983. The CPI-U adopted this method in 1983, and the two series are identical after that date.

5. Unless otherwise noted, the numbers in this chapter are based on the author's tabulations of the March CPS microdata files. Tables are available from the author.

6. Hispanics are not identified separately in the 1970 CPS; hence we cannot compare them with other ethnic groups in 1969.

7. Overall average family income in each year is the weighted average of mean total family incomes for married couples and single parents (Figures 10 and 11), weighted by their respective shares of all families. Disproportionate growth in the upper tail of the income distribution pulls up the mean more than the median.

8. Top-coded values of income components were multiplied by 1.45 so that the means would not be underestimated.

9. For estimates of changes in family incomes using a broader definition of income, see Levy (1996).

10. How could earnings increase more than wages, while hours declined? This reflects the correlation between changes in hours and wages in the population, and the fact that earnings are the product of the wage rate times hours worked. Mathematically, the average of a product is not equal to the product of the averages.

11. Hispanics are not identified separately in the 1970 CPS; hence we cannot compare them with other ethnic groups in 1969.

12. Robinson and Godbey (1997), Table 3. The child care category in the time diaries only includes time spent on direct caregiving. Any changes in time parents spend with children while they are primarily engaged in another activity, such as cooking, cleaning, or shopping, are not reflected in the time-use data.

13. Data on alternative work arrangements come from the 1991 and 1997 May supplements to the CPS, as reported in Council of Economic Advisers (1999), p. 14.

References

Bachu, Amara, and Martin O'Connell. 2000. *Fertility of American Women: June 1998.* Current Population Reports, P20-526, U.S. Census Bureau, Washington, D.C., September.

Blau, Francine. 1998. "Trends in the Well-Being of American Women, 1990-1995." *Journal of Economic Literature* 36(March): 112–165.

Council of Economic Advisers. 1999. *Families and the Labor Market, 1969-1999: Analyzing the "Time Crunch."* Report, Washington, D.C., May. Available on the Internet at http://clinton4.nara.gov/WH/EOP/CEA/html/whitepapers.html.

Danziger, Sheldon, and Deborah Reed. 1997. "Working Longer and Earning More: The Changing Contribution of Wives' Earnings to Family Income." Unpublished manuscript, University of Michigan, February.

Juhn, Chinhui, and Kevin Murphy. 1997. "Wage Inequality and Family Labor Supply." *Journal of Labor Economics* 15(1), part 1: 72–97.

Levy, Frank. 1996. "Where Did All the Money Go? A Layman's Guide to Recent Trends in U.S. Living Standards." Working Paper 96-008, MIT Industrial Performance Center, July.

McKinnon, Jesse, and Karen Humes. 2000. *The Black Population in the United States: March 1999.* Current Population Reports, P20-530, U.S. Census Bureau, Washington, D.C., September.

Robinson, John, and Geoffrey Godbey. 1997. *Time for Life: The Surprising Ways Americans Use their Time.* State College: Pennsylvania State University Press.

Sandberg, John F., and Sandra L. Hofferth. 2001. *Changes in Children's Time with Parents, U.S. 1981–1997.* PSC Research Report No. 01-475, Population Studies Center, University of Michigan, May.

Schmidley, A. Dianne, and Campbell Gibson. 1999. *Profile of the Foreign-Born Population in the United States: 1997.* Current Population Reports, P23-195, U.S. Census Bureau, Washington, D.C., August.

Therrien, Melissa, and Roberto R. Ramirez. 2001. *The Hispanic Population in the United States: March 2000.* Current Population Reports, P20-535, U.S. Census Bureau, Washington, D.C., March.

U.S. Census Bureau. 2001a. *Historical Income Tables—People, Table P-38. Full-Time, Year-round Workers (All Races) by Median Earnings and Sex: 1960 to 1999.* Last revised February 7, 2001. Available on the Internet at http://www.census.gov/hhes/income/histinc/p38.html.

———. 2001b. *Historical Income Tables—People, Table P-38A. Full-Time, Year-round White Workers by Median Earnings and Sex: 1967 to 1999.* Last revised February 7, 2001. Available on the Internet at http://www.census.gov/hhes/income/histinc/p38a.html.

———. 2001c. *Historical Income Tables—People, Table P-38B. Full-Time, Year-round Black Workers by Median Earnings and Sex: 1967 to 1999.* Last revised February 7, 2001. Available on the Internet at http://www.census.gov/hhes/income/histinc/p38b.html.

———. 2001d. *Historical Income Tables—People, Table P-38D. Full-Time, Year-round Workers of Hispanic Origin by Median Earnings and Sex:*

1974 to 1999. Last revised February, 7 2001.   Available on the Internet at
http://www.census.gov/hhes/income/histinc/p38d.html.

4

Fertility, Public Policy, and Mothers in the Labor Force

Susan L. Averett
Lafayette College

INTRODUCTION

Few policy debates draw more attention or more heated discussion than those concerning population policy. Many countries have struggled to influence their birth rates. Countries such as Germany, France, and Sweden have instigated a variety of policies to deal with low birth rates, while other countries such as India, Singapore, and China have had varying degrees of success with policies to reduce their birth rates. The United States has also experienced below-replacement fertility in recent decades, but it has not implemented explicit pronatalist policies as many other industrialized countries have done. Most U.S. population policy is centered on controlling immigration. Nevertheless, recent research on the economics of fertility has demonstrated that the United States does indeed have policies that have an impact, whether intended or not, on the birth rate. For example, recent research has determined that tax exemptions for children, welfare benefits, family planning funded by Medicaid benefits, and company-provided maternity leave all exert statistically significant effects on fertility. Interestingly, the policies that lower the cost of raising a child (such as taxes and maternity leave), were not specifically designed to affect fertility, whereas the polices that have an antinatalist effect (such as certain provisions related to welfare reform and Medicaid-funded family planning) were in fact designed to lower birth rates among specific subgroups of the population.

At the same time that some of these policies have been enacted, expanded, and/or modified, the U.S. total fertility rate has remained remarkably constant and hovers just below replacement (Figure 1).[1] The constant overall total fertility rate does mask the fact that the teen-age birth rate in the United States is quite high and has only recently shown signs of declining (Figure 2).[2] Although the overall birth rate in the United States has remained fairly constant over the past two decades, during this time period there has been tremendous growth in the labor force participation of women, particularly women with young children (Figure 3). As of 1994, the labor force participation rate of married women with preschool-aged children was virtually identical to that of married women with older children (Hotz, Klerman, and Willis, 1997). This increase in the labor force participation rate of married women with children has generated much discussion as to how government and business can and/or should ease the dual burden of work and family that falls primarily on women.

In this chapter I explore two related areas of research. The first is the effect of public policies on the birth rate in the United States. I focus on the fertility effects of taxes, welfare, Medicaid, and maternity leave. Because these policies have the potential to influence birth rates, and because economists view fertility and labor force participa-

Figure 1 Total Fertility Rate

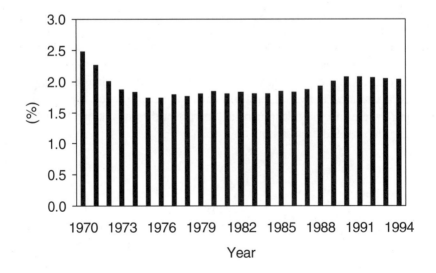

Figure 2 Teen Birth Rate per 1,000 Women in Specified Group

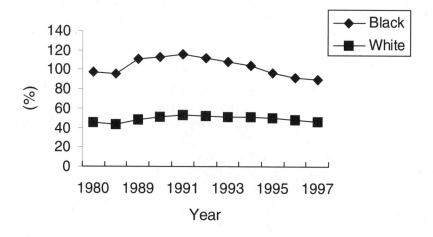

Figure 3 Female Labor Force Participation Rates

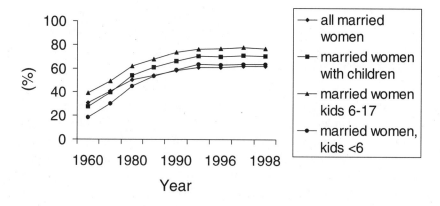

tion as simultaneous, I also examine the labor force participation of mothers. In particular, I focus on two issues related to mothers in the labor force. The first revolves around continued reports in the popular press that professional women are fleeing the workforce due to conflicting work and family roles. Although most of the evidence on this topic is anecdotal, it has the potential to lead employers to believe that women with children are not committed to the workforce, perhaps leading employers to be less willing to invest in women. To address this issue, I report on some of my own research that examines whether or not professional women are leaving the labor force and returning to the home to care for their children. The second issue I explore is the family pay gap—the earnings differential between women with and without children. While the gender pay differential has received much attention and has narrowed recently, the family pay gap has received scant attention and has grown in recent decades.

This chapter is organized as follows. In the next section, I outline the basic economic theory behind the economics of fertility. Following that I discuss the effects of various public policies on the fertility of U.S. women. In the next section I discuss both the issue of women returning from the workforce to care for children and the family pay gap that exists between women with and without children. In the final section I offer some concluding remarks.

THE ECONOMICS OF FERTILITY

To understand how public policies such as income taxes, welfare reform, and maternity leave can affect fertility, it is useful to begin with some economic theory. My discussion is short and nontechnical.[3] The economic model of fertility is essentially an extension of neoclassical demand theory. Parents are assumed to receive utility from children (or child quality) as well as from other goods. Parents are also assumed to behave rationally and to be perfect contraceptors; that is, they are effective users of contraception. Children (or child quality) can be either produced primarily at home (home-cooked meals, parental child care) or with goods bought from the market (restaurant meals, prepared foods, and purchased child care). Parents maximize their utility subject to a full-income budget constraint where full income is defined as that amount of income the household would have if it devoted all available time to working. The full-income budget constraint thus explicitly includes the hourly wage rate as the opportunity cost of time. Therefore, the model recognizes that not only are there explicit costs of raising a child (diapers, food, etc.), there is a significant time cost or opportunity cost associated with raising a child. This time cost is traditionally borne by the mother.

The model leads to the prediction that the demand for children is a function of income, prices, tastes, and preferences. Theoretically, there is some ambiguity surrounding the potential impact of women's wages on fertility due to competing income and price effects. The general expectation, however, is that fertility will be negatively associated with a woman's wage rate because traditionally women have borne the time cost of children. In fact, Schultz (1994) has noted that virtually all economic studies of fertility have found a negative relationship between women's earnings or women's education (a good proxy for earnings) and fertility.

In the following section I review and discuss research that examines several specific policies and their effects on fertility in the United States. All of these policies change the budget constraint facing the family because they change the price of a child. Thus, as parents weigh the costs and benefits of an additional child, they are assumed to take into account the change in costs and/or benefits imposed by the policy under consideration.

PUBLIC POLICY AND FERTILITY

Taxes and Fertility

As noted above, the economic model of fertility suggests that couples weigh the financial costs of raising a child together with the time inputs of parents against the utility gains from having children. Tax and transfer payments that vary with family size alter these costs and benefits and thus are expected to have an effect on the demand for children. Politicians have often stated that increasing the personal exemption in the U.S. income tax would decrease the cost of a child. In the late 1980s, several economists began noting that tax variables, by changing the "cost" of a child, could have an impact on fertility. In one of the first papers in this vein, Whittington, Alm, and Peters (1990) examined the possibility of a causal relationship between the value of the personal exemption in the U.S. income tax and the U.S. total fertility rate.

The personal exemption, a feature of the income tax system since 1913, was instituted to provide relief for low-income families from the burden of taxation. Thus, the original intent of the personal exemption was not to subsidize births (Pechman 1983). Unlike other policies that might affect fertility, the personal exemption is an ongoing subsidy that families receive each year they claim the child as a dependent on their income tax form. For most families, this subsidy lasts for at least 18 years. In 1994, the U.S. Department of Agriculture estimated that the out-of-pocket expenditures required to raise a child to age 18 amounted to $136,320. Whittington, Alm, and Peters report that the personal exemption actually covers between 4 and 9 percent of the out-of-pocket costs of a child. Clearly this is not an inconsequential subsidy.

Using aggregate time-series data for the United States from the period 1913–1984, Whittington, Alm, and Peters model the general fertility rate (the birth rate per thousand women between the ages of 15 and 44) as a function of the tax value of the personal exemption, women's average wages, and a variety of other regressors. They confirm that the dependent exemption has a positive and statistically significant effect on the total fertility rate. In related work, Whittington (1992) demonstrates that the time series finding of a statistically significant and positive link between fertility and the personal exemption also holds in the cross section.

This subsidy to fertility does have some distributional effects, as it is primarily geared to middle-income families. Low-income families often are outside of the tax system due to the zero bracket amounts and the fact that high-income families typically do not qualify for the personal exemption.

Another feature of the U.S. income tax code that has the potential to increase fertility is the earned income tax credit (EITC). Unlike the personal exemption, the EITC is targeted to low-income women. There is ample evidence that this credit increases labor supply, but no one has yet examined its possible fertility incentive. However, because it is a refundable tax credit for individuals who have dependent children in the household, it has the potential to alter fertility. It is a more complicated subsidy than the personal exemption because although it provides a subsidy to families with dependent children, it also increases wage rates. Given the regular empirical observation that higher wages reduce fertility, the EITC may also work to reduce fertility to the extent that it increases the time cost of having children. Thus, any empirical study that looks at the relationship between earned income taxes and fertility must take account of these two offsetting effects and sort out their impact on fertility. It is worth noting that the potential distributional impact of this policy is quite different from the dependent exemption because the EITC is targeted specifically to low-income families. It is possible, though unconfirmed empirically, that this subsidy could provide a birth incentive to low-income families.

There are other features of the tax code that may also have an effect on fertility. The child and dependent care tax provides a tax credit worth up to 30 percent of a family's child care costs in a given year. The impact of this subsidy on births is indirect because in order to be eligible for this subsidy, the family must be using some mode of paid child care. Also, because this subsidy lowers the cost of child care, thus increasing wage rates and thereby labor supply, it may in fact, like EITC, have the effect of dampening the birth rate. To date, there has been no research that examines this issue, though there is a body of work that has examined the link between child care costs and fertility. Connelly (1991) surmises that the actual effect of the child and dependent care tax credit on fertility is small.

Welfare and Fertility

Although some people are skeptical about whether or not economic variables play a role in the complex decision to have a child, one need look no further than those involved in the welfare reform movement to find policymakers and voters who believe that economic incentives can and do affect fertility. Welfare reform has received much recent attention since 1996, when President Clinton signed into law the Personal Responsibility and Work Opportunity Reconciliation Act (PRWORA). This represented a large change in welfare programs.

Prior to this time, welfare benefits were available to women with dependent children, allowing low-income women to stay home with their children. But increasing out-of-wedlock births and a changing political climate have changed society's—and policymakers'—views of women on welfare. Perceptions that married women not on welfare are increasingly opting to work full time and utilize day care services has also contributed to the idea that poor women should not have the option to raise their children at home while collecting welfare benefits (Cohen and Bianchi 1999).

When PRWORA passed, the Aid to Families with Dependent Children program (AFDC) was renamed Temporary Assistance to Needy Families (TANF). The TANF program was designed to deal specifically with several perceived shortcomings of the old AFDC system. Women receiving TANF are now subject to time limits and work requirements. In addition, teen mothers must live with a parent or other responsible adult to receive benefits. Child support enforcement was also increased. Furthermore, states are now allowed to implement family caps, i.e., deny an increase in monthly welfare benefits to women who have more children while on welfare. It is this latter provision that is the focus of my discussion.

Under the old welfare system, in most states the monthly AFDC payment increased with the number of children in the family. Many policymakers and researchers expressed concern that this encouraged women on welfare to have more children in order to collect more money each month. Under TANF, states may now implement a family cap that denies increased benefits to children born to a recipient parent. Mandated family caps at the federal level were not instituted under TANF primarily because abortion foes raised concerns that family caps would encourage more abortions (Klerman 1998). Prior to TANF, states could apply for a federal waiver if they wanted to implement a family cap. New Jersey was the first to do so in 1992, and Arkansas followed quickly. As of July 2000, 23 states had family caps.

There have been numerous studies of the effects of AFDC on fertility. These are summarized in Moffitt (1992, 1998). The early literature suggests only a weak link between AFDC and fertility (Moffitt 1992; Schultz 1994). Later work, reviewed in Moffitt (1998), does find evidence of a link between welfare payments and fertility, although the magnitude varies widely. Because these studies examine first births and do not distinguish between welfare recipients and non-recipients, they cannot be used to assess the consequences of a family cap. Economists have only recently examined the potential effect of family caps on the birth rate.

Researchers who study family caps and fertility rely on statewide variation in the monthly level of incremental AFDC benefits (rather than the total benefit) to determine if there is an effect on fertility. Because family caps only apply to women currently on welfare, it is typical to limit the sample for analysis to those women receiving welfare benefits. One important issue that must be addressed by all researchers looking into the effects of welfare payments on fertility is the issue of how states choose their policies. If policies were randomly assigned, it would be appropriate simply to regress fertility on the incremental benefit levels in each state, controlling for other demographic and personal characteristics of the woman. However, policies are not randomly assigned; they are generated by the democratic process. For example, states with particularly high abortion rates may adopt policies to curb these rates. Similarly, states with many welfare recipients may have generous welfare benefits primarily because voters in those states believe in supporting single parents, i.e., it is not the policy that is causing the behavior but the behavior is causing the policy. Of course, policymakers are interested in how exogenous changes in policy affect behavior. Such exogenous variation in policy can be difficult to isolate. As Klerman (1998) states: "A crucial methodological issue is thus how to estimate the true effect of the law while controlling for persistent differences in the states adopting policies and other social changes" (p. 118). The approach most often used, *state fixed effects* (Moffitt 1992), is to include a dummy variable for each state in the model. Often, adding state fixed effects to the model deletes any statistically significant effect of incremental welfare payments on fertility.

Although there is some evidence to suggest that births to recipients may be reduced with the imposition of a family cap, many policymakers are concerned about whether or not lower incremental benefits reduce births by reducing pregnancies or by increasing abortions. Most proponents of family caps contend that any reduction in births to recipient mothers will be accomplished through a decrease in pregnancies. However, a reduction in births may instead result from an increase in abortions. This possibility has prompted concern by the public, the popular press, and policymakers, and as mentioned earlier, it was one of the reasons family caps were not mandated at the federal level (Klerman 1998). Clearly, given the controversy surrounding abortion in the United States, this is an important issue to research. Klerman (1998) presents evidence from the sociology and social psychology literature indicating that many teenage women will resort to abortion when faced with the realities of PRWORA. In other words, rather than becoming better contraceptors, teenagers are more likely to react to a family cap by increasing abortions. However, researchers at the Alan Guttmacher Institute argue that teenagers are better contraceptors than many believe—their figures indicate that nearly 60 percent of poor and low-income teenage women and about 75 percent of higher-income adolescent women use some method of contraception the first time they have sexual intercourse and that an even higher proportions use it on an ongoing basis (Alan Guttmacher Institute 1998).

By exploiting state differences in payments under AFDC, Argys, Averett, and Rees (2000) examine the link between incremental welfare benefits, pregnancy, and pregnancy resolution among welfare recipients. We use a sample from the National Longitudinal Survey of Youth (NLSY) of unmarried women who received AFDC income for at least one year between 1979 and 1991. We estimate a bivariate probit model of the determinants of pregnancy while on AFDC and, conditional on becoming pregnant, the probability of obtaining an abortion. Estimates from our model indicate that there is no evidence that family caps will increase abortions. We do find some effect of family caps on pregnancy. The pregnancy effect is most pronounced for women with three or more children. Contrary to what other studies have found, we found no difference in the responses of white, black, and Hispanic recipients to incremental benefit levels.

However, one problem confronting any research that uses microlevel data to examine abortions is that the incidence of abortion is severely underreported in most survey data sets. Several researchers have expressed concern about underreporting of abortions in survey data. Lundberg and Plotnick (1995) state that white premarital teens in the youth cohort of the NLSY report 33 percent fewer abortions than medical records would lead one to expect. Black teenaged women were even less likely to report their abortions, with nearly 80 percent unreported. These findings are similar to those of Jones and Forrest (1992), who suggest that the underreporting may be related to marital status as well as race. Argys, Averett, and Rees (2000) also note the severe underreporting of abortions in the NLSY data set but note that as long as the underreporting is not systematically related to the explanatory variables in the model, the estimates will be unbiased. Klerman (1998) argues that such severe underreporting makes the estimation of policy effects from survey data impossible. His review of the available evidence of the effect of welfare reform on abortion also indicates that there is no effect of AFDC payments on abortion. It should be noted that the studies he reviewed did not focus specifically on a welfare population and so did not examine the effects of incremental AFDC benefits; i.e., family caps.

Family caps are an antinatalist policy directed at low-income women. Although family caps apply to only a small fraction of women in their childbearing ages, they bring up many social and political questions. Donovan (1995) notes that despite considerable debate about family caps, there is almost nothing known about the consequences for the families who have another child and are denied benefits. Will they be able to pay their rent? Will their children go hungry? These are also concerns voiced by the Catholic Church (Pear 1995). These issues have not yet been dealt with, but welfare reform speeds ahead with states reporting dramatic declines in their welfare caseloads (Council of Economic Advisers, 1999). There is considerable debate over whether or not the declines in welfare caseloads are due entirely to welfare reform or to the strong economy that has prevailed during the late 1990s. At least one study reports that an economic downturn could increase welfare roles substantially (Black, McKinnish, and Sanders 2000).

Another policy in the United States that affects the fertility of low-income women in a potentially antinatalist way is the money that is allocated to family planning efforts. In particular, the Medicaid program subsidizes family planning for low-income women. Surprisingly, there is not much recent work on the link between Medicaid-funded family planning efforts and fertility. A study by Mellor (1998) is a notable exception. She uses data from Medicaid claims for the state of Maryland. Although her results are specific to Medicaid recipients in Maryland, they provide some of the best evidence we have of the effect of federally funded family planning on the fertility of low-income women. Women who are on Medicaid receive family planning services, and by federal law they pay no co-payments on prescription family planning services or supplies (unlike women who use private health insurance, which often does not cover items such as birth control pills). Mellor's results indicate that women who are exposed to federally funded family planning through the Medicaid program have a lower probability of having a birth. The magnitude of the effect is larger than that found by earlier researchers. She argues that this is because her method takes into account the potential correlation between the unobservable determinants of family planning use and fertility.

It is interesting to note that policymakers have zeroed in on family caps as an effective way to reduce the fertility of welfare recipients despite the fact that the evidence is unclear as to whether or not family caps are effective. Mellor's work suggests that an effective way to reduce births among this population is to provide family planning services. Family planning programs, unlike family caps, are not discussed as much among policymakers.

Maternity Leave and Fertility

Given the dramatic increase in the labor force participation rate of mothers documented earlier, there has been increased policy attention on how firms and/or government can accommodate the needs of women for both leave time after childbirth and stable job status. In the United States, the debate over maternity leave largely centered around the role of government in family decisions, and this public debate ultimately led to the adoption of the federal Family and Medical Leave Act (FMLA) in 1993. The FMLA guarantees 12 weeks of unpaid parental (meaning both women and men are eligible) leave to most employees of relatively large firms. This offers substantial job protection to some parents following the birth of their children. It is, however, estimated that this legislation will only pertain to about half of U.S. workers due to coverage limitations, primarily because only firms employing more than 50 persons are required to comply (Joesch 1995). Further, no firms are required by law to offer *paid* parental leave. Some firms did offer maternity leave (largely unpaid) prior to the passage of the FMLA, but it has generally been a benefit offered only to employees at large firms that pay relatively high wages (Kamerman and Kahn 1997; Phillips 2001).

The expansion of parental leave laws to provide coverage for all workers, and the requirement that such leaves be compensated, remain issues of national debate. Advocates emphasize that the United States is the only industrialized country that does not guarantee paid maternity leave (Kamerman and Kahn 1991).   Critics argue that expanded leave will result in higher costs for employers, as they must hire replacement workers and/or deal with greater employee absenteeism, and that these costs will be particularly devastating to small firms (Trzcinski and Finn-Stevenson 1991; Kamerman and Kahn 1997). Another cost concern is that women will be induced to have more births because maternity leave lowers the cost of a child, and that this increased fertility will exacerbate the financial burden on firms. Opponents also argue that actual costs combined with employers' fears of increasing fertility will harm the position of women in the labor force because employers will steer away from hiring women in their reproductive years. This could stigmatize working mothers. To deal rationally with these concerns, it is crucial to understand whether women increase births in response to employer-provided maternity leave. There is a growing literature exploring the impact of maternity leave on labor supply patterns and earnings in the United States (Phillips 2001; Waldfogel 1997a; Klerman and Leibowitz 1997, 1998). To date, only two papers examine the impact of maternity leave on births among U.S. women. The paucity of empirical work on this issue is surprising given that the fertility concerns are an often-cited reason for not offering such leave.

In a cross-national study on maternity leave and demographic outcomes, Winegarden and Bracy (1995) estimate a model relating paid maternity leave to three demographic outcomes: infant mortality rate, labor force participation rates of women of childbearing age, and fertility. They find that paid maternity leave decreases infant mortality rates and raises female labor force participation. Interestingly, despite the fact that paid maternity leave in many of the countries in his data set was actually instituted as a policy to increase fertility rates, it has not had that effect because the increase in female labor force participation subsequently reduces fertility. Their research underscores the importance of considering the simultaneous nature of many demographic and labor force decisions.

In Averett and Whittington (2001), we model the effect of employer-provided maternity leave on the probability of a birth for U.S. women and find that firm-provided maternity leave can in fact have a rather large influence on births, particularly second and higher-order births. We hypothesize that the temporal ordering of events among working women is as follows. A woman first selects her job with or without maternity leave as a benefit. Then, she either has a birth or not. Because of the waiting period often required of benefits packages, a woman may be in a position for a year or more before having access to maternity benefits. It therefore seems unlikely, though not impossible, that a woman would move into a position with maternity leave because she is already pregnant. Because maternity leave is not a benefit explicitly available with every job or firm, women may seek it out as a particular characteristic of their desired job just as people may search for other job benefits such as flexible schedules, tuition remission, or health insurance. Determining the impact of maternity leave on fertility therefore requires explicit recognition of this potential sorting into jobs with maternity leave based on anticipated fertility, and it is not as straightforward as the dependent exemption or the family caps discussed earlier.

In order to determine the effect of maternity leave on births, we estimate two equations: 1) the probability of a woman selecting a job with maternity leave, and 2) the probability of having a birth. The probability of choosing a maternity leave job is a function of her desired fertility, economic and social conditions in the area in which she resides, and personal characteristics that affect her tastes, prices, and income. The probability of a birth is posited to be a function of her wages, nonearned income, maternity leave, and tastes and preferences for children. Thus, the effect of maternity leave on fertility is actually the sum of two effects: the indirect effect of desired fertility on the probability of being in a maternity leave job, and the direct effect of maternity leave on the probability of a birth.

Maternity leave lowers the cost of a birth whether it is paid or unpaid leave, and lowering the cost of childbirth creates a fertility incentive. Hoem (1990) and Walker (1991), in analyses of maternity leave in Sweden, note that this positive incentive may be dampened if there is any sort of minimum work period required in order to accrue full benefits. If workers are required to meet a minimum term of employment before becoming fully vested in maternity benefits, the existence of maternity leave might actually *increase* the time to birth, thereby decreasing the probability of a birth in early years. Further, a woman with maternity leave benefits may be a more highly valued employee of the firm, and may have a stronger, unobserved attachment to the labor force, making a birth less probable than for a woman with a lower labor force attachment (and no maternity leave). Thus, the direct effect of maternity leave on fertility can not be determined *a priori*.

We estimate our model using data from the NLSY and find no evidence that working women who desire children self-select into firms offering maternity leave. Once in a firm, however, maternity leave does appear to directly increase the probability of a birth for working women, at least for women with at least one child already, and the effect is actually quite substantial. The following calculation provides an estimate of the potential magnitude of the effect we found. In 1995, the Census Bureau reported that 2,034,000 working women aged 15–44 had births, a rate of about 5.65 percent among the roughly 36 million working women in that age group. If all working women were given access to guaranteed maternity leave, the birth probability would presumably rise only among the 23.5 percent (based on our sample) who previously had not benefited from such a policy, and, again, likely only for higher-order births. Thus, increased coverage might result in an additional 118,000 births. This would increase the overall rough birth probability among working women aged 15–44 to just under 6 percent, an increase of 0.4 percentage points. Any change in the fertility or labor market behavior of women not in the labor market resulting from expanded maternity leave policy is not included in this estimated birth increase and, of course, as Winegarden and Bracy note, the labor market effects have the potential to dampen the fertility effects. In other words, if maternity leave encourages more women to work, it may end up decreasing births. Because the NLSY does not collect data on maternity leave coverage for women who are not in the labor force, we cannot empirically test at the individual level whether or not women who are offered maternity leave are more likely to work.

The evidence reviewed above suggests that several public policies in the United States influence the birth rate. The personal exemption in the U.S. tax system provides a subsidy to children, and it is confirmed that it has a positive impact on births, both in time-series and cross-section models. The effects of welfare payments on fertility, and specifically family caps, provide more modest evidence on the impact of these payments on fertility. To date there is no evidence that family caps will increase abortions, though further study on this issue is warranted. Employer-provided maternity leave is also found to influence the birth rate, particularly for higher-order births. Clearly, the government has intervened in the family. The distributional effect of these policies is worth noting. The pronatalist subsidies are for the most part geared to middle- and high-income women, while the antinatalist programs clearly target low-income women.

The focus on fertility in welfare reform and the push to get welfare mothers into the paid labor force, as well as continued debate about whether the United States should mandate paid maternity leave, brings up an often-debated issue. Is there more that the government should do to help women balance family and career? In the next section, I focus on how mothers fare in the labor force.

BALANCING WORK AND FAMILY IN THE UNITED STATES

The research reviewed above demonstrates that government policy has the potential to impact personal decisions such as fertility. Fertility rates in the United States have remained fairly constant over the past 20 years, as shown earlier in Figure 1. During this same time frame, female labor force participation, particularly among women with infants, has grown dramatically. For example, in 1975, the labor force participation rate of married women with children under one year old was 30.8 percent. By 1998 this number had climbed to 61.8 percent, a growth rate of just over 100 percent. We can expect even bigger growth in the labor force participation of low-income women with preschool-aged children, as welfare reforms continue to push this group of mothers into the labor force. The balance between family and job responsibilities is increasingly the focus of many researchers and policymakers. In 1989, the late Felice Schwartz wrote an article for the *Harvard Business Review* where she argued that employers should put family-focused women on a slower career track and keep women who viewed their careers as coming first on the fast track (Schwartz 1989). Though she didn't use the term "mommy track," it quickly became a popular buzzword. Now, over a decade after she suggested this, there is still debate over the merits of mommy tracking.

In recent years, the popular press in the United States has repeatedly profiled professional women who have elected to leave the labor force to devote their full-time energies to child rearing. This is an extreme version of the mommy track, as these women supposedly elect to leave the labor force entirely rather than to simply cut back on hours and attempt to balance job and family responsibilities. The conclusion in mainstream media is often that mothers have tired of trying to be "superwomen" and have decided that high achievement in the labor force is not compatible with a successful home life (Deogun 1997; Jacobs 1994; Morin 1991; Tailor 1991). Goldin (1998) notes that for young women with college degrees, the difficulty in balancing work and family remains a major concern. Others have suggested that the relative prosperity of the 1990s has afforded women the choice to stay home and that many career-minded professional women are exercising their freedom to choose, i.e., they are not necessarily tired of trying to juggle family and home life, they just want to stay home (Quinn 2000; Jeffrey 2000). It is not, of course, just professional women who struggle with finding a balance between work and family. Sicherman (1996), for example, found that a higher proportion of women than men leave their jobs for nonmarket reasons, such as household duties and family illness. Culpan, Akdag, and Cindogvlu (1996), Wentling (1996), and Gordon and Whelan (1998), among others, also present evidence indicating that family concerns play a large role in women's career satisfaction, retention, and achievement.

The effect of repeated mass media articles in this vein has been to leave the impression that women currently entering professions are less committed to a long-term career than were women in previous decades. This anecdotal impression can be used in some dangerous inferences about the validity of investing in women. Of further concern, policymakers could conclude that aggressive pursuit of policy options protecting women's positions in the labor market is unnecessary. Statistical discrimination with respect to women based on their potential labor force attachment may flourish if employers fear that a woman's odds of returning to the home are greater than they were in the past.

Interestingly, this set of articles appears at a time when the majority of the empirical evidence suggests that women with children have a heightened attachment to the labor force. The growth in the labor force participation rate of women has slowed in the 1990s, but there is no reason to believe that these rates will fall.[4] Furthermore, as mentioned earlier, the labor force participation rate of mothers of preschool-aged children has climbed more rapidly than the overall female labor force participation rate. Women are not only working more, they are making inroads into traditionally male-dominated occupations. For example, data from the Current Population Survey indicate that in 1999, 46.7 percent of full-time wage and salary workers in executive, administrative, and managerial occupations were women, up from 34.2 percent in 1983 (U.S. Department of Labor 2000). Women are also working later into pregnancy, and they return to work more quickly after childbirth (Wentling 1996). In fact, Klerman and Leibowitz (1994) report that about half of all women return to work by the time their child is four months old. They also note that women returning to work closely after the birth of a child account for nearly all of the women who will return to work that first year. Hayghe and Bianchi (1994) report that married mothers are twice as likely to work full time all year than their predecessors of 20 years ago. Thus, the commitment to the workforce on the part of mothers appears stronger than ever.

Despite the considerable anecdotal evidence surrounding this issue, there is little empirical evidence that professional women are leaving the workplace. Whittington, Averett, and Anderson (2000) examine this issue more closely, and the results of that research are summarized here. To determine whether or not professional women are leaving the workforce more frequently than in years past, we use a sample of managerial and professional women from the Panel Survey of Income Dynamics, and we estimate the probability of withdrawing from the labor force at one-, two- and five-year intervals after the birth of a child. Our sample consists of married women who report that they are working in a professional, managerial, or technical position in the year preceding a birth during the years 1968–1992. Because previous research by Shapiro and Mott (1994) and Klerman and Leibowitz (1994) highlights the importance of making the distinction between being employed and working, we use several definitions of withdrawal from the labor force.   For example, many women do not withdraw completely from the labor force after giving birth but are still employed by their firms even though they may be out on leave. Likewise, a woman might be currently out of work but still consider herself attached to the labor market and plan to return.   The distinction between work and employment is therefore important in understanding women's employment behavior following childbirth.

It is also important to control for other factors that may affect labor force attachment, such as earnings, work experience, and husband's earnings, since others have found that these factors influence whether or not women will return to work after the birth of a child (Desai and Waite 1991; Klerman and Leibowitz 1994).   Therefore, we regress each measure of labor force withdrawal on the set of covariates, described above, and control for the time period when the woman gave birth. Our results indicate that women who gave birth in recent years are more likely to report zero hours of work two years after the birth of a child when compared with women who gave birth earlier in the sample period. Thus, we find some support for the supposition that more professional women are opting to stay home and raise children in lieu of aggressively pursuing their careers. We do not find any differences by cohort, indicating that this phenomenon cuts across women of all childbearing ages. However, our results are not robust across different measures of labor force withdrawal, nor are they consistent across postpartum time intervals. One possible explanation for our findings is that women of later childbirth periods may now face a more flexible workplace that permits them to cut back on their hours or take an extended leave, perhaps without pay, while still maintaining their attachment to the workforce. There is some anecdotal evidence that this is the case and that the strong economy of the late 1990s has given women more flexibility in the labor market (Wylie 2000).

There is some support, albeit weak, for the conjecture that professional women are opting to leave the workforce. Why? Several factors have been put forth to explain this exodus. Perhaps the most salient is the existence of the glass ceiling. Although women have made great inroads in the labor market, there is still a considerable gap at the top. Myerson and Fletcher (2000) report that women still comprise only 10 percent of senior management positions at Fortune 500 companies.

The data are not broken down by child status, but it is safe to say that considerably few of the women who are senior corporate managers have children, or at least young children.

Another explanation for this phenomenon may be the pay differential that still exists between men and women. Currently women earn 76 percent of what men earn. Although women are better represented in the top-paying occupations, within those broad occupational categories women are much less likely to be employed in the higher-paying occupations. For example, in the professional specialty occupations, where women earn the most, they are much less likely to be employed as engineers and mathematical and computer scientists and more likely to work as teachers (except college and university) and registered nurses (U.S. Department of Labor 2000). The median weekly earnings of teachers is $671 and the median earnings of registered nurses is $739 while the median weekly earnings for engineers and mathematical and computer scientists is between $900 and $1,000 (Bowler 1999).

What may be a more compelling reason for women with children to opt out of the labor force may not be the gender pay gap but the family pay gap. The family pay gap is defined as the difference in pay between women with and without children. Economists have documented for many years that women with children earn less than women without children, while this is typically not found for men. In fact, there is some evidence that marriage (though not necessarily children) raises men's earnings (Korenman and Neumark 1991). Waldfogel (1998) examines this issue more closely and finds that the family gap for women has been widening at the same time the gender pay gap has been decreasing. For example, she notes that women without children earned 68.4 percent of what a man earned in 1978, but that by 1994 that figure had risen to 81.3 percent. The same figures for a woman with children were 62.5 percent and 73.4 percent, respectively. However, a married woman with children under the age of six earned only 67 percent of what a married man with children under the age of six earned, while women with no children under age 18 earned 83 percent of what a man with no children under age 18 earned. These figures are unadjusted for differences in human capital investment and occupation. Thus, they may be misleading if men and women have different productivity characteristics; i.e., it may be that women with children have less education or less work experience on average. However, the family penalty remains even when other important wage determining variables such as education, ability, previous work experience, and other factors have been controlled.

To provide an estimate of the magnitude of the effect of children on men's and women's wages, I use data from the 1993 wave of the NLSY.[5] I use separate samples of men and women, as is typical when estimating human capital wage functions. Limiting my sample to high school graduates, I estimate a human capital earnings function, controlling for the usual set of human capital, demographic, and location variables. One advantage of using the NLSY is that it provides information on weekly work experience and has an ability indicator; all respondents were administered the Armed Forces Qualifications Test in 1980 (AFQT), which is a test of academic ability. The dependent variable in the analysis is the natural log of hourly earnings. As shown in Table 1, it is clear that the presence of a child lowers earnings by nearly 8 percent for women and that the effect is statistically significant. For men, children *increase* their earnings by 6 percent, and the effect is statistically significant. These figures are even more dramatic when I limit my analysis sample to those women and men who are in managerial and professional occupations. Having a child lowers a female manager's earnings by 15 percent while having a child has virtually no impact on the earnings of a male manager. Like Korenman and Neumark (1991), I find married men to have higher earnings than nonmarried men.[6]

Waldfogel (1998) notes that there are several theories put forth to explain the lower earnings of mothers. The most obvious, and the one for which we have virtually no empirical evidence, is discrimination. It is possible that women with children face statistical discrimination— employers believe they are less likely to be attached to the labor force and are thus reluctant to invest in them. Another theory put forth by Becker (1985) states that the earnings penalty faced by mothers is due to lower effort. Women with children and families exert less effort on the job and thus earn lower wages. If such effort is unmeasured when estimating a human capital earnings function, the resulting wage penalty may not reflect the effect of the child per se but may simply be a difference in effort. However, recent research that carefully accounts for effort has generally not confirmed that this is the case (McLennan 2000).

Table 1 Log Wage Regressions for Men and Women from 1993 NLSY

Variable	All women	All men	Women managers	Men managers
Constant	2.261***	1.961***	2.570***	0.646
	(0.171)	(0.177)	(0.419)	(0.469)
AFQT score	0.454***	0.517***	0.526***	0.500***
(percentile)	(0.000)	(0.000)	(0.100)	(0.100)
Child	−0.079***	0.056***	−0.150***	0.005
	(0.023)	(0.021)	(0.049)	(0.052)
Black	0.076***	−0.028	−0.012	0.007
	(0.025)	(0.023)	(0.060)	(0.064)
Married	0.091	0.140***	0.038	0.155**
	(0.026)	(0.025)	(0.057)	(0.061)
Separated/div./	0.049*	0.024	0.066	0.030
widowed	(0.030)	(0.029)	(0.011)	(0.090)
Age	−0.023***	−0.016***	−0.020	0.021
	(0.005)	(0.005)	(0.011)	(0.012)
Experience	0.028**	0.057***	0.008	0.117***
	(0.013)	(0.015)	(0.037)	(0.040)
Experience^2	0.001*	−0.000	0.001	−0.000**
	(0.001)	(0.001)	(0.002)	(0.002)
Has Bachelor's	0.263***	0.247***	0.109**	0.163***
degree	(0.030)	(0.029)	(0.051)	(0.051)
Has Associate's	0.139***	0.101***	0.102	0.001
degree	(0.033)	(0.036)	(0.067)	(0.082)
Adjusted R^2	0.257	0.237	0.151	0.149
N	2,997	3,416	782	713

NOTE: Standard errors are in parentheses. All models include controls for region of residence (3 dummy variables) and a control for center city residence. *** = Statistically significant at the 1% level; ** = statistically significant at the 5% level; * = statistically significant at the 10% level.

Waldfogel (1998), in her study of the family gap, notes that job-protected maternity leave has the potential to close the family wage gap. She finds that women who have job protected maternity leave experience less of a wage penalty to having children. Waldfogel argues that this is because maternity leave coverage raises the probability that women return to their previous employers after childbirth.

Having women return to their previous employers is advantageous, she argues, because this job continuity provides women the opportunity to receive general and firm-specific training and work experience that will boost their pay. This opportunity is typically lost when a woman has to return to a completely new employer or position following child-birth. She also notes that child care and other family friendly policies also have the potential to close the family pay gap.

CONCLUSIONS

The study of the economics of fertility has consistently found that economic variables play an important role in determining fertility rates. Despite experiencing below replacement level fertility, the United States does not have any explicit policies designed to influence fertility rates. However, there are several public policies that affect the fertility decisions of families. Most of these policies are antinatalist at the low end of the income distribution and are more pronatalist to women at the upper end of the income distribution. Some of these policies grew out of concern over the high fertility rates of certain groups of the popula-tion, such as welfare recipients. Other policies, such as maternity leave, were not designed to influence fertility but rather to help women combine family and work responsibilities.

The growing involvement of women in work outside the home has focused attention on the status of women, particularly mothers, in the labor force. It is clear that working women are an entrenched feature of the labor market. There is evidence that family-friendly policies, such as job-protected maternity leave, will help put them on more equal ground economically. Although women have made sizable progress in the labor force, there are still barriers. Women still earn only 76 percent of what men earn. They still work in female-domi-nated jobs, and they are still underrepresented in upper management. Women with children earn less than comparably qualified women without children. With many former welfare recipients poised to enter the labor market, it is of increasing importance to examine the delicate balance between work and family that many women must maintain. If professional women find the dual task of family and career daunting, it must seem impossible to a low-skilled woman facing the prospect of a low-wage job and childcare costs. For former welfare recipients, childcare issues will be at the forefront as these women scramble to find affordable, quality child care for their children.

Notes

1. The total fertility rate is defined as the number of births that 1,000 women would have in their lifetime if at each year they experienced the birth rates occurring in the specified year. A total fertility rate of 2.11 represents replacement level fertility at current mortality rates.
2. High teenage birth rates have been a concern of policymakers for some time in the United States. I do not discuss them specifically, except in the context of welfare reform. Readers interested in examining some of the issues should see Levine (2000).
3. For an excellent and more technical and detailed presentation of the models, see Hotz, Klerman, and Willis (1997). For those interested in reading some of the seminal work, see Schultz (1974).
4. Hayghe (1994) notes that although there was a break in the data between 1989 and 1991, there is no evidence to support the assertion that the labor force participation rate of women has leveled off or is going to fall.
5. Economists emphasize the simultaneous nature of the labor supply and fertility decisions. In these models I make no attempt to control for the endogeneity of children. Failure to control for this likely biases the coefficient on children upward. See Angrist and Evans (1998) for a model that does account for the endogeneity of children. See Waldfogel (1997b) for a comprehensive examination of the effect of children on women's earnings.
6. I do not control for occupation in these models, although controlling for occupation (in models not presented here) does not reduce the child penalty. This suggests that women with children are not necessarily in lower-paying occupations.

References

The Alan Guttmacher Institute. 1998. *Teenage Pregnancy and the Welfare Reform Debate.* New York.

Angrist, Joshua, and William N. Evans. 1998. "Children and Their Parents' Labor Supply: Evidence from Exogenous Variation in Family Size." *American Economic Review* 88(3): 450–477.

Argys, Laura, Susan Averett, and Daniel Rees. 2000. "Welfare Generosity, Pregnancies and Abortions Among Unmarried Recipients." *Journal of Population Economics* 13(4): 569–594.

Averett, Susan L., and Leslie A. Whittington. 2001. "Does Maternity Leave Induce Births?" *Southern Economic Journal* 68(2): 403–417.

Becker, Gary. 1985. "Human Capital, Effort and the Sexual Division of Labor." *Journal of Labor Economics* 3(1): S33–S58.

Black, Dan, T. McKinnish, and Seth Sanders. 2000. "Are We Understanding the Impact of Economic Conditions on Welfare Roles?" Syracuse University Policy Brief.

Bowler, Mary. 1999. "Women's Earnings: An Overview." *Monthly Labor Review* 122(12): 13–21.

Cohen, Philip, and Suzanne Bianchi. 1999. "Marriage, Children, and Women's Employment: What Do We Know?" *Monthly Labor Review* 122(12): 22–31.

Connelly, R. 1991. "The Importance of Child Care Costs to Women's Decision Making." In *The Economics of Child Care,* D. Blau ed. New York: Russell Sage.

Council of Economic Advisers. 1999. "The Effects of Welfare Policy and the Economic Expansion on Welfare Caseloads: An Update." www.whitehouse.gov. Accessed December 2000.

Culpan, O., F. Akdag, and D. Cindogvlu. 1996. "Women in Banking: A Comparative Perspective on the Integration Myth." *International Journal of Manpower* 13(1) 33–40.

Deogun, Nikhil. 1997. "Top PepsiCo Executive Picks Family Over Job." *The Wall Street Journal.* September 24, p. B1.

Desai, S., and L. Waite. 1991. "Women's Employment During Pregnancy and After the First Birth: Occupational Characteristics and Work Commitment." *American Sociological Review* 56(August): 551–566.

Donovan, Patricia. 1995. "The 'Family Cap': A Popular but Unproven Method of Welfare Reform." *Family Planning Perspectives.* 27(4): 166–171.

Goldin, C. 1998. "Career and Family: College Women Look to the Past." In *Gender and Family Issues in the Workplace,* Blau, F. and R. Ehrenberg, eds. New York: Russell Sage, pp. 20–56.

Gordon, J., and K. Whelan. 1998. "Successful Professional Women in Midlife: How Organizations Can More Effectively Understand and Respond to the Challenges." *Academy of Management Executives* 12(1): 8–27.

Hayghe, Howard V. 1994. "Are Women Leaving the Labor Force?" *Monthly Labor Review* 117(7): 37–39.

Hayghe, Howard V., and Suzanne M. Bianchi. 1994. "Married Mothers' Work Patterns: The Job-Family Compromise." *Monthly Labor Review* 17(6): 24–30.

Hoem, Jan M. 1990. "Social Policy and Recent Fertility Change in Sweden." *Population and Development Review* 16(4): 735–748.

Hotz, Joseph, Jacob Klerman, and Robert Willis. 1997. "The Economics of Fertility in Developed Countries." In *Handbook of Population and Family Economics,* Rosenzweig and Stark, eds. New York: Elsevier, pp.276–342.

Jacobs, Deborah L. 1994. "Back From the Mommy Track." *The New York Times.* October 9.

Jeffrey, Nancy Ann. 2000. "The New Economy Family." *The Wall Street Journal.* Weekend Journal, September 8.

Joesch, Jutta. 1995. "Paid Leave and the Timing of Women's Employment Surrounding Birth." Working Paper No 95-10, Center for Studies in Demography and Ecology, University of Washington.

Jones, Elise, and Jacqueline Forrest. 1992. "Underreporting of Abortion in Surveys of U.S. Women: 1976–1988." *Demography.* 29(1): 113–126.

Kamerman, Sheila B., and Alfred J. Kahn. 1991. "A. U.S. Policy Challenge." In *Child Care, Parental Leave, and the Under 3s,* Sheila B. Kamerman and Alfred J. Kahn, eds. New York: Auburn House, pp. 1–22.

————. 1997. "United States." In *Family Change and Family Policies in Great Britain, Canada, New Zealand and the United States,* Sheila B. Kamerman and Alfred J. Kahn, eds. Oxford: Clarendon Press, pp. 305–421.

Klerman, Jacob. 1998. "Welfare Reform and Abortion." In *Welfare, The Family, and Reproductive Behavior: Research Perspectives,* Washington, D.C.: National Academy Press.

Klerman, J., and A. Leibowitz. 1994. "The Work-Employment Distinction Among New Mothers." *Journal of Human Resources* 29(2): 277–303.

————. 1997. "Labor Supply Effects of State Maternity Leave Legislation." In *Gender and Family Issues in the Workplace,* Francine D. Blau and Ronald C. Ehrenberg, eds. New York: Russell Sage Foundation, pp. 65–85.

————. 1998. "FMLA and the Labor Supply of New Mothers: Evidence from the June CPS." Paper presented at the Annual Meeting of the Population Association of America, 1998.

Korenman, Sanders, and David Neumark. 1991. "Does Marriage Really Make Men More Productive?" *Journal of Human Resources* 26(2): 282–307.

Levine, Phillip B. 2000. "The Sexual Activity and Birth Control Use of American Teenagers." Working paper, The National Bureau of Economic Research, Washington, D.C.

Lundberg, Shelly, and Robert D. Plotnick. 1995. "Adolescent Premarital Childbearing: Do Economic Incentives Matter?" *Journal of Labor Economics* 13(2): 177–200.

McLennan, Michele. 2000. "Does Household Labour Impact Market Wages?" *Applied Economics* 32(12): 1541–1557.

Mellor, Jennifer. 1998. "The Effect of Family Planning Programs on the Fertility of Welfare Recipients: Evidence from Medicaid Claims." *Journal of Human Resources* 33(4): 866–895.

Moffitt, Robert. 1992. "Incentive Effects of the U.S. Welfare System: A Review." *Journal of Economic Literature* 30(1): 1–61.

Moffitt, Robert. 1998. "The Effect of Welfare on Marriage and Fertility." In *Welfare, the Family, and Reproductive Behavior*, Robert Moffitt, ed. Washington D.C.: National Academy Press, pp. 50–97.

Morin, Richard. 1991. "The Trend that Wasn't; Are Moms Leaving Work? Or Did the Dip Deceive?" *The Washington Post.* July 14.

Meyerson, Debra E.,and Joyce K. Fletcher. 2000. "A Modest Manifesto for Shattering the Glass Ceiling." *Harvard Business Review* 7(1): 126–136.

Pear, Robert. 1995. "Catholic Bishops Challenge Pieces of Welfare Bill." *The New York Times.* Sunday, March 19, p. A1.

Pechman, Joseph. 1983. *Federal Tax Policy.* Washington, D.C.: The Brookings Institution.

Phillips, Katherin Ross. 2001. "Working for All Families? Family Leave Policies in the United States." Chapter 6 in this volume.

Quinn, Jane Bryant. 2000. "Revisiting the Mommy Track." *Newsweek.* July 17, p. 44.

Schultz, Paul T. 1994. "Marital Status and Fertility in the United States: Welfare and Labor Market Effects." *The Journal of Human Resources* 29(3): 637–669.

Schultz, T.W. 1974. *The Economics of the Family, Marriage, Children and Human Capital.* Chicago, IL: National Bureau of Economic Research.

Schwartz, Felice. 1989. "Management Women and the New Facts of Life." *Harvard Business Review*(67)1: 65–77.

Shapiro, David, and Frank L. Mott. 1994. "Long-Term Employment and Earnings of Women in Relation to Employment Behavior Surrounding the First Birth." *Journal of Human Resources* 29(2): 248–275.

Sicherman, N. 1996. "Gender Differences in Departures from a Large Firm." *Industrial and Labor Relations Review* 49(3): 484–505.

Tailor, Paul. 1991. "Work Losing Romanticized Aura of the '80s; Polls Show Shift Toward Emphasis on Motherhood and Home." *The Washington Post*. May 12.

Trzcinski, Eileen, and Matia Finn-Stevenson. 1991. "A Response to Arguments Against Mandated Parental Leave: Findings from the Connecticut Survey of Parental Leave Policies." *Journal of Marriage and the Family* 53(2): 445–460.

U.S. Department of Labor. 2000. "Highlights of Women's Earnings in 1999." Bureau of Labor Statistics. Report 943.

Waldfogel, Jane. 1997a. "Working Mothers Then and Now: A Cross-Cohort Analysis of the Effects of Maternity Leave on Women's Pay." In *Gender and Family Issues in the Workplace*, Francine Blau and Ronald Ehrenberg, eds. Russell Sage Foundation: New York: 92–126.

———. 1997b. "The Wage Effects of Children." *American Sociological Review* 62: 209–217.

———. 1998. "Understanding the 'Family Gap' in Pay for Women with Children." *Journal of Economic Perspectives* 12(1):137–156.

Walkcr, James R. 1991. "Maternity Benefits, Fertility, and Female Labor Supply." Paper presented at the Fourth Annual Conference of the European Society for Population Economics, Pisa, Italy, June 6–8, 1991.

Wentling, Rose Mary. 1996. "A Study of the Career Development and Aspirations of Women in Middle Management." *Human Resource Development Quarterly* 7(3): 253–270.

Winegarden, C.R., and P.M. Bracy. 1995. "Demographic Consequences of Maternal-Leave Programs in Industrial Countries: Evidence from Fixed Effects Models." *Southern Economic Journal* 61(4): 1020–1035.

Whittington, Leslie A. 1992. "Taxes and the Family: The Impact of the Tax Exemption for Dependents on Marital Fertility." *Demography* 29(2): 215–226.

Whittington, Leslie A., James R. Alm, and H. Elizabeth Peters. 1990. "The Personal Exemption and Fertility: Implicit Pronatalist Policy in the U.S." *American Economic Review* 80(3): 545–556.

Whittington, Leslie A., Susan L. Averett, and Donna M. Anderson. 2000. "Choosing Children Over Career? A Cross-Cohort Exploration of the Postpartum Labor Force Behavior of Professional Women." *Population Research and Policy Review* 19(4): 339–355.

Wylie, Margie. 2000. "Taking the Mommy Track: Strong Competition for Executives in the Internet Industry Allows Working Mothers to Demand and Win Job Flexibility." *The Cleveland Plain Dealer*. June 13, p. 5f.

5

How Family Structure Affects Labor Market Outcomes

Joyce P. Jacobsen
Wesleyan University

The chapter title appears self-evident—of course family structure matters! Surely the quirks and turns of one's personal life—which for almost everyone is inextricably commingled with their family's lives—would have measurable effects on almost everything that you do, including whether or not you work, how much you earn, and a host of other facts about your work experience. It would have seemed unreasonable to have instead titled this essay: How family structure *doesn't* affect labor market outcomes.

But it turns out that uncovering exactly how family structure matters is not a trivial undertaking. Because economics is not in general an experimental science, it is difficult to make a convincing argument that family structure matters, holding all other factors constant that are potentially correlated with family structure. We can't just randomly assign people to different family structures in which to spend their lives and see what happens. Untangling the actual "family assignment" mechanism from the outcome is a difficult problem that researchers have tackled using a number of methodological approaches. We will gauge how convincing their solutions are, and the degree to which taking this problem seriously modifies the raw numbers that we see in the unmassaged data.

In this chapter I will first define family structure and labor market outcomes, and show you examples of the kinds of patterns that lead people to believe that family structure influences labor market outcomes. I will briefly outline the theoretical reasoning that leads one to believe that family structure would matter, as well as the reasoning that can lead one to believe that it matters less than most people might think. In the next section I consider the evidence from a number of studies that attempt to measure carefully the effects of family structure—particularly marital status and presence or absence of children in the household—on labor force participation and earnings measures. I conclude by looking at a few studies that consider aspects of family structure more broadly defined, and by discussing whether the results shown have relevance for any particular policy initiatives.

WHAT IS FAMILY STRUCTURE?

Family structure can refer to anything about a person's past and present living conditions and relational structure. But we need a narrow definition of a family to understand the way data are commonly collected by statistical agencies. Let's look at the U.S. Census Bureau/ Department of Labor definition, which relies on both relation and co-residence: "A family is a group of two persons or more (one of whom is the householder) residing together and related by birth, marriage, or adoption. All such persons (including related subfamily members) are considered as members of one family." Hence, while a household "consists of all the persons who occupy a house, an apartment, or other group of rooms, or a room, which constitutes a housing unit," a family household "is a household maintained by a family (as defined above), and may include among the household members any unrelated persons (unrelated subfamily members and/or unrelated individuals) who may be residing there" (U.S. Department of Labor 1995).

Using these definitions, in order to see how families might vary and how they overlap with households, consider the concrete case of the United States population as of March 1999 (most of the results I present in this paper are based on U.S. data, and the remaining results come from other developed countries; I do not argue that the results are necessarily more widely applicable). Let us consider three widespread phenomena (and their absence): people living more than one to a household, people living with someone they are married to, and people living with their own children (under 18) in a household.

Figure 1 displays the proportions of households that fall into these types of categories and shows how these numbers vary by sex. The convention is to define either an individual or a married couple as the householder(s), i.e., the person(s) in whose name(s) the housing unit is owned or rented. We see that out of the 100 million U.S. households in

Figure 1 The Proportional Distribution of U.S. Households, by Various Characteristics, 1999

103,874,000 households (all percentages are out of this total)

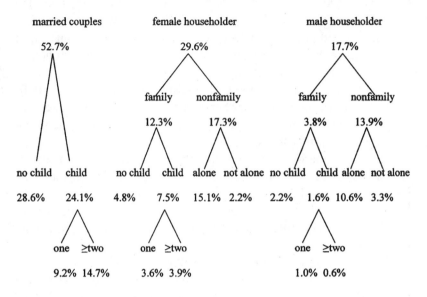

NOTE: "Child" refers to own child under 18.
SOURCE: U.S. Department of Commerce, Bureau of the Census (2000, Tables 60, 62, 65).

1999, slightly more than half were headed by a married couple and more than one-quarter were female-headed; the remaining 18 percent were male-headed households. Female- and male-headed households can be further subdivided into family and nonfamily households, of which a majority are nonfamily households (i.e., do not contain related persons). Nonfamily households can consist of one or more nonrelated persons; 5.5 percent of all households consisted of unrelated persons, while over a quarter of all households (25.7 percent) contained only one person. Hence, about two-thirds of all households are family households. Only 1.9 percent of married couples do not have their own household, so being married is highly related to maintaining a family household (U.S. Department of Commerce, Bureau of the Census 2000, Table 60). Neither households nor families are particularly large in general: the average household size is 2.61 persons and the average family size is 3.18 persons (U.S. Department of Commerce, Bureau of the Census 2000, Table 60). Notably, the idealized view of the "nuclear family" as consisting of a married couple with two or more children is found in less than 15 percent of households—about one of every seven—although potentially many more of us are in such households for at least some percentage of our lives.

Even while maintaining the U.S. statistical agencies' narrow definition of a family, one might further refine one's view of living conditions that might matter in a number of ways. For instance, one might examine more closely the different types of "nonmarriage": cohabitation; previously married, but now widowed, divorced, or separated; living alone; or living with other persons in a nonsexual relationship. One might also want to know if previous structure has lasting effects; for example, does a divorced person appear quite different from a widowed person, and do both of those appear different from someone who has never married?

One might also want to know more about the type of marriage that one is in. Do the spouses largely conform to traditional roles within the marriage? Do both spouses work? Which spouse earns more? One might also want to know more about the age structure of the family, including the ages of the children and, potentially, also of the spouses.

One might also be interested in how one relates to other family members who may reside in other households. One might be in a caregiver relationship with an elderly and/or disabled family member who lives elsewhere. One might have a dependent who does not live in the household but who still represents some level of financial (and emotional) obligation.

In addition, one might wonder how family structure in the past affects one today. Perhaps one's siblings continue to exert an influence even after one no longer interacts with them daily. Children, grandchildren, parents, siblings, aunts, uncles, cousins, and in-laws all potentially affect your current life in measurable ways, whether or not you currently interact with them regularly.

WHAT ARE LABOR MARKET OUTCOMES?

What sorts of outcomes might we measure? As an economist, my mind naturally turns to observable, independently verifiable outcomes such as earnings and hours worked. For the purposes of this chapter, we will consider three outcome measures: two measures of labor supply, labor force participation (work/not work), and hours worked; and hourly earnings. This by no means exhausts the range of outcomes. Netz and Haveman (1999) make a good case for including family structure variables as potential controls/predictors for studying a wide range of labor market outcomes—such as unemployment duration—where researchers have not normally thought to include such variables. However, much of the extant empirical work has in fact considered one or more of these three outcomes.

First let's see what the raw numbers can show us. Table 1 shows some calculations for prime-age adults (ages 25 to 54) for the United States in March 1999. For this group, consider first their labor force participation rate (i.e., the proportion that is either currently employed or actively looking for paid work). Women are less likely to be participating in the labor force if married, while the opposite holds for men. The hours effect for those who are working goes in a similar direction. Women in larger families, measured by either number of persons or number of children, have reduced participation and hours. Men in larger families have higher participation but little variation in hours, and men in very large families have reduced values for both measures. Married persons earn more per hour worked than do unmarried persons, but the effect appears to be much stronger for men than for women. Women in larger families have substantially reduced hourly earnings, while for men in very large families hourly earnings first rise and then fall, with little difference in the midrange (two to five people; one to three children).

Before taking these hourly earnings rates as given, we might first want to consider how aggregation affects these patterns. For instance, maybe married and unmarried persons have very different demographic characteristics, like their age distribution (which could relate both to generic lifecycle differences and differences by birth cohort). By showing results only for persons between 25 and 54 in Table 1, I

Table 1 Labor Market Outcome for Prime Age Workers, by Sex and Family Structure Characteristics

	Women					Men				
	Labor force participation rates (%)	Weekly hours	Hourly earnings ($)	Family earnings ($)	n	Labor force participation rates	Weekly hours	Hourly earnings ($)	Family earnings ($)	n
All persons	77	38	11.53	43,000	29,573	92	44	15.38	46,000	27,360
Currently married	74	37	11.54	56,000	19,339	94	45	16.83	56,000	18,126
Currently unmarried	82	40	11.11	23,000	10,234	87	43	12.82	30,000	9,234
Number of persons in family										
1	85	41	12.82	24,000	4,319	89	44	13.75	27,000	5,955
2	81	39	12.02	44,000	6,925	90	44	15.38	50,000	5,423
3	79	38	11.43	47,000	6,280	92	44	15.38	53,000	5,178
4	74	36	11.11	54,000	6,762	95	45	16.53	58,000	6,066
5	68	35	10.00	52,000	3,360	94	45	16.35	56,000	3,042
≥6	62	35	8.65	44,000	1,927	90	44	13.00	48,000	1,696
Number of children in family										
0	81	40	12.02	40,000	13,912	89	44	14.42	40,000	14,552
1	79	38	11.54	47,000	5,980	94	45	16.48	55,000	4,741

2	74	36	10.99	48,000	6,050	96	45	16.83	55,000	5,110
3	66	34	9.62	42,000	2,610	95	45	16.73	51,000	2,164
≥4	55	33	7.92	32,000	1,021	92	46	14.42	41,000	793

NOTE: Hours and hourly earnings are calculated only for those persons reporting nonzero values.

SOURCE: Author's calculations using data from the U.S. Department of Commerce, Bureau of the Census (1999).

have already controlled for age to some degree, but it could be done more carefully. It turns out that the same patterns appear if I look within narrower age ranges, say 10-year age ranges (25–34, 35–44, 45–54). I might also want to consider different types of non-marriedness, such as widowed, divorced, separated, or never married. For these middle-aged persons, the differences in outcomes between these categories is quite small; current marital status (rather than past marital history) becomes the important distinction.

We might also want to control simultaneously for marital status and family size using a multiple regression framework to see the effects of each factor while holding constant the other factor. Let's consider the family structure effects on earnings using this idea. Applying a simple model to the hourly earnings data described in Table 1 (using the natural log of hourly earnings as the dependent variable, and with no other controls except for age and age-squared), for men, being married is associated with a 22 percent higher earnings rate, while the number of children has no effect; for women, being married is associated with 5 percent higher hourly earnings, while *each child* is associated with a 6 percent drop in hourly earnings.

WHY ARE FAMILY STRUCTURE AND LABOR MARKET OUTCOMES RELATED?

For both men and women, but particularly for men, marriage is associated with higher hourly earnings. For women, each additional child is associated with lower hourly earnings. Why do we see these patterns?

I derived these percentages from a very sparse regression specification, in which many of the usual variables that we would associate with earnings rates, like one's education and work experience, were missing. So one obvious answer is that marriage and number of children are serving as proxies for a number of omitted variables that are directly related to productivity as rewarded in the labor market. Indeed, these variables are often included in regressions, particularly for data sets where not many other variables are available, in order to serve as proxy for these other measures (Hill 1979). These might include labor force attachment, pre- and postschool human capital investments, stability, restrictions on work location and hours, absenteeism, and turnover. Hence, studies that include a longer list of control variables should drive these family effects toward zero.

One problem with this approach is that not all variables that are related to labor market productivity are available in the kind of data sets that are generally available. For instance, many measures of ability or effort might be important to employers but are not collected in surveys. The person surveyed might not even know how other people view his or her actions and abilities. And these unobservable differences across persons are potentially correlated with whether or not they marry and how many children they have.

We could get away from the omitted variable problem completely if we could randomly assign people to marry or not marry (and whom to marry!), and randomly assign people to have different numbers of children. Indeed, if you think that marriage markets are like a lottery in the sense that love strikes almost randomly, this would not be a problem. But as we will see shortly, there is evidence that people do not randomly marry with respect to economic factors. Indeed, exactly the opposite occurs: currently, potential high earners are likely to marry other high earners. Similarly, if you think that the number of children a family has is basically an act of God, then we have a natural experiment as to how children affect labor market outcomes.

Another problem is that even if you find that persons with certain features are both more likely to marry and to make more money, this could still be due to either effort or discrimination. How could this be? Let's consider the theoretical arguments for the two main phenomena we have observed with respect to earnings: 1) women with children earn less than women without children, and 2) married men earn more than unmarried men. This will also help us understand why labor force participation and hours might vary in the ways shown in Table 1.

One of the main arguments economists will give for why people marry (or at least for why they live together) is that marriage allows for gains in household output due to increasing the spouses' ability to specialize. Hence, a couple's total household output would likely be greater than the sum of what they were able to produce separately, particularly if they can increasingly specialize over the course of the marriage. If women have comparative advantage (i.e., are relatively better) at home production, they will be less likely to work for pay after marriage. Children raise the value of time spent in home production, so children can amplify this effect considerably. Meanwhile, married men can specialize in market-related human capital investments, thereby increasing their productivity over time. In some cases, the woman may choose to devote her time to forwarding the man's career, again in cases where this time investment has a higher payoff than either her working in the market herself, or spending the time in other forms of nonmarket production.

But what about cases where we observe both spouses working for pay? The argument must then be extended to say that women with children are less productive than both childless women and all men per hour worked in the market. This could happen for a number of reasons. They may be directly less productive because they have invested less in the past in market-related human capital. Many women take time off to raise children before reentering the labor market; hence, women on average have less total work experience than do men, as well as less time with their current employer. Even if they had the same amount of total work experience or total job tenure, leaving the labor force for more than six months in order to raise children is in and of itself associated with lower hourly earnings (Jacobsen and Levin 1995), possibly because their human capital has depreciated during their absence from the labor market. Also, anticipating discontinuous employment, they may have invested in forms of human capital that were less likely to depreciate, or that might be more useful in a variety of geographic locations if they will be moving to further their spouse's career.

Another possibility is that rather than less human capital being applied per hour of work, women with children are applying less effort per hour of work. If at-home production requires a certain amount of one's fixed daily stock of energy, the person doing more at-home production may exert less effort per hour of market production. Note that the opposite effect potentially occurs for men who are freed from responsibilities for at-home production, and for men whose wives are actively supporting their career (throwing parties for their colleagues and customers, accompanying them on trips), the employer may really be receiving twice the effort per hour of work.

Alternatively, women may be applying equal amounts of both effort and human capital per hour but may be constrained in their selection of jobs to those that have flexible and/or part-time hours. It is well documented that such jobs generally have lower earnings rates, potentially because these are desirable features, or because such jobs are less valuable to employers. Hence women's desire to reduce hours of paid work so as to spend more time in nonmarket production leads to their lower earnings per hour. Meanwhile, married men may select jobs that have fewer amenities (including but not limited to flexibility) but higher wages (Reed and Harford 1989). In other words, there exist jobs with higher pay but fewer amenities and jobs with lower pay but greater amenities, and people sort systematically between them based on gender and family structure.

That outlines the basic neoclassical economic argument for why marital status and number of children would have effects on labor force participation, hours, and earnings: marriage and children alter one's relative productivity between home and work and potentially one's choice of pecuniary and nonpecuniary amenities related to work. Note, however, that for any point made above, it is possible to make an alternative argument that marital status and number of children either won't or will matter in the opposite direction. For example, the potential endogeneity of the human capital investment decision will make it hard to measure the full effects of marriage and children on current earnings; there may be no current effect, but past anticipation of becoming married with children will have led women to invest in less human capital than they would have otherwise. However, if most women plan to (or assume that they will) become married and have children, this will depress women's earnings relative to men but will have little effect on the differential earnings between married and unmarried women.

It is also possible to derive alternative explanations for why these phenomena occur. In particular, marriage and children might alter not only one's choice set but also one's preferences. For example, married men might work harder because now there are other people—people whom they care about—whose well-being is affected by their level of income.

Another alternative explanation is that society (broadly defined, but also narrowly defined as employers) prefers certain familial configurations to others, potentially for economic reasons, and attempts to reward persons who conform to these norms while penalizing those who do not. So married men, particularly those with stay-at-home wives, receive higher pay raises and more frequent promotions. Meanwhile, women find it difficult to combine work with home duties, and employers make it no easier for them. Employers may favor the traditional style of marriage out of simple prejudice and a desire to replicate the male-dominated management structure that they have become accustomed to. An alternative, statistical, discrimination theory would be that employers use family structure as a proxy for the unobservable factors of effort, emotional stability, and turnover (i.e., marriage and children are good for men but bad for women).

To sum up, we see that there are four main categories of explanations for why there might be differences in earnings and labor market work associated with changes in family structure: both absolute and relative productivity in market work may be affected; preferences are altered; trade-offs between higher pay and higher job amenities are in part based on family structure; and discrimination—either prejudicial or statistical—occurs. It is not necessary to pick one of these explanations over the others; rather, they might all be operating simultaneously, each accounting for some proportion of the wage and employment differences.

In addition, we see that there are a number of reasons why it would be hard to observe these effects cleanly using nonexperimental data: selection into marriage and into child raising must be taken account of to the degree that both observable and nonobservable factors affecting selection are correlated with either productivity or preferences regarding market versus nonmarket work. Various studies have taken these different theoretical and empirical considerations seriously. We will see how they have reduced—or strengthened—the marital wage premium for men and the family wage penalty for women. I will briefly summarize the range of results and sum up my views in each of these two cases.

THE EFFECTS OF MARRIAGE

Many studies have considered the puzzle of why married men earn more. This premium varies across studies from zero to 30 percent, depending on the particular data set and time period studied and on the nature of the empirical methodology. The premium clearly persists if standard, observable controls for productivity are added, such as educational attainment and actual or estimated work experience (Hill 1979), and is larger for persons in professional and managerial occupations (Pfeffer and Ross 1982). Following people over time, which is a way of controlling for unobservable variables, indicates that wages rise after marriage, and that the managerial and professional effect appears to be related to receiving higher performance ratings and therefore being more likely to be promoted to higher, better-paying jobs (Korenman and Neumark 1991). These results are all consistent with both the higher productivity and the discrimination arguments.

However, in controlling for unobservables that affect both wages and marital status, a number of studies have found that the marital status premium is greatly reduced or eradicated (Cohen and Haberfeld 1991; Cornwell and Rupert 1995; Nakosteen and Zimmer 1987, 1997; Loh 1996). There is also some reason to believe that the marital premium is declining over time. This may be related not only to reduced differences in human capital investment between married and unmarried men (Blackburn and Korenman 1994), but also to reduced specialization in market work during marriage, possibly related to rising divorce probabilities (Gray 1997; Gray and Vanderhart 2000). On the other hand, a recent study using the 1999 March CPS finds that even after controlling for endogeneity of marital status, married men have a 13 percent wage premium (Chun and Lee 2001).

A number of studies (Chalmers 1996; Jacobsen and Rayack 1996; Blackaby, Carlin, and Murphy 1998; Hotchkiss and Moore 1999; Chun and Lee 2001) have considered differences among married men in the marital wage premium, specifically how their spouse's work hours might affect the wage premium. These studies generally find differences, after controlling for observable productivity-related characteristics, of approximately 15 percent between married men whose wives do not work and married men whose wives work full time. By the effort argument put forth above, we should observe that a man who has a nonworking wife will have higher wages because his wife is free to dedicate relatively more time to furthering his career, either directly through career-related activities, or indirectly by freeing him from almost all home production obligations. However, this effect could also be due to one or both of two alternative explanations: the assortative mating effect, in this case leading to matches between men who have high market productivity and women who have high nonmarket productivity; and the endogeneity of spousal work hours. In other words, if a man is a high earner, his wife reduces her paid work time, even potentially increasing leisure time rather than home production. Jacobsen and Rayack (1996) find that the effect disappears in U.S. data (the Panel Study of Income Dynamics) when either of these two alternative explanations is controlled for and Chalmers (1996) finds that controlling for endogeneity alone is enough to eradicate the phenomenon in five different data sets (data from the Luxembourg Income Study for Australia, Canada, Netherlands, Sweden, and the United States). However, Hotchkiss and Moore (1999) find that the effect persists in U.S. data for managerial occupations, as do Blackaby, Carlin, and Murphy (1998) for a United Kingdom data set; and Chun and Lee (2001) find that the effect persists in a broader sample of men in the United States even when controlling simultaneously for marital endogeneity and hours endogeneity.

The effects of marriage on women have received less attention, but the slight positive wage premium related to marriage appears to persist even when heterogeneity and endogeneity bias are accounted for. Neumark and Korenman (1994), using data on sisters to control for these factors, find a positive marriage premium for white women. Using a different data set, however, they previously found no direct effect on women's wages (Korenman and Neumark 1992). Jacobsen and Levin (1995) find no statistically significant effect of current marital status once fairly detailed controls for work experience, including intermittency spells, are included.

The difficulty of considering all explanations simultaneously, using a data set that has good controls for human capital variables (particularly work experience and intermittency measures) and controlling for heterogeneity and endogeneity, shows up in these differing results. Based on the current studies, I am not completely willing to concede that there is currently in the United States any marital wage premium for men or women. This is clearly an area of active research, and one where more research, including more replicative and summarizing studies, is needed.

THE EFFECTS OF CHILDREN

A topic that has received even more ink and has been equally controversial has been the effects of childbearing and child raising on female labor supply and earnings. The reduced earnings effect operates largely through the reduced labor supply effect and is more relevant for total family earnings than on hourly earnings. However, there does appear to be an effect even on the hourly earnings rate, as we saw in Table 1. Waldfogel (1998) argues that there is still an effect in U.S. data, and that the penalty is in the 10 to 15 percent range in comparing women with children to women with no children. Again, as with the men, we might first want to know how adding traditional observable controls for productivity affects this finding. Indeed, studies that have added such controls, particularly for work experience and job tenure, have reduced considerably the effect of children on wage, adding credence to the idea that the presence of children in the household is to a large degree a proxy for these direct productivity effects (Hill 1979; Jacobsen and Levin 1995; Lundberg and Rose 2000). But how to treat the endogeneity of work experience and job tenure is contentious. Korenman and Neumark (1992) argue that if this endogeneity is not controlled for (i.e., the effects of children in reducing these measures is taken into account), the negative effect of children on wages is understated.

One study that considered the family gap across seven developed countries (Australia, Canada, the United Kingdom, the United States, Germany, Finland, and Sweden) finds much variation in the effects of children on both employment and wages, with the largest wage penalty for children in the United Kingdom (Harkness and Waldfogel 1999). In the United Kingdom, the presence of children still strongly inhibits full-time employment, and the low pay in part-time work appears to be an important explanation of the "family gap" in wages (Joshi, Macran, and Dex 1996; Joshi et al. 1999). These findings raise the question of how institutional differences across countries can affect this gap, potentially through the indirect link of children to wages through reducing labor force attachment.

A method that avoids the endogeneity and heterogeneity problems is to use natural experiments involving multiple births and the gender mix of children. In other words, to the extent that multiple births are not planned and that people aim to have children of specific genders and therefore might have additional children if the first one or two are not of the desired sex, these outcomes cause increases in the number of children in a family over what the family might have desired. These studies generally find rather small additional child effects on both labor supply and earnings (Rosenzweig and Wolpin 2000). Another study in this vein (Jacobsen, Pearce, and Rosenbloom 1999) finds small effects of total fertility on married women's labor supply and earnings, depressing labor supply by 2.5 percent and hours worked by two per week per additional child, and essentially no effect on hourly earnings, which is consistent with the raw numbers in Table 1.

Another method that attempts to measure directly whether time and effort spent on household production affects labor market outcomes is to measure the effects of household production directly. Studies using a variety of econometric specifications (Hersch 1991a,b; Hersch and Stratton 1997, 2002) have indeed found a significant negative effect on women's wages of time spent on housework; approximately 10 weekly hours of housework reduces hourly earnings by about 2 percent (Stratton 2001). Housework hours variations by marital status are fairly large for women and may even be relevant in explaining the negative wage differentials related to the presence of children (although this particular specification was not tested by the mentioned studies). In contrast, results have been inconclusive for men, with the possibility of a smaller negative impact or no effect (Hersch 1991b; Hersch and Stratton 1997, 2002), while the other study (Hersch 1991a) actually found a slight positive effect of time spent on housework on men's wages. Notably, Hersch and Stratton (2000) find that married and single men spend virtually the same amount of time on home production, "albeit on different types of housework"; not surprisingly, they also find no effect of housework on the marital wage premium for men.

Note that while one interpretation of these results is that time spent on housework reduces one's ability to do well in the labor market, another interpretation is that time spent on housework is a proxy negatively correlated with drive or ambition in the labor market. In addition, the negative effect can operate through creation of a constraint (i.e., picking part-time positions with lower wage rate) rather than through effort or flextime (Stratton 2001).

Another line of research has attempted to measure attitudes toward family life directly and use these attitudinal measures as control variables. Interestingly, while Rose and Winkler (2000) find that women's inclinations toward traditional roles in the family are correlated with lower labor force attachment and earnings, Cappelli, Constantine, and Chadwick (2000) find that persons placing a high priority on family before entering the labor market earn more; women who place a high priority on family do not suffer in terms of subsequent earnings.

Fewer studies have bothered to consider the effects of children on men, given the apparent absence of a strong effect in the raw data on either hours or earnings (although Hersch [1991b] finds a positive effect of presence of children on both male and female wages). However, Carlin and Flood (1997) consider this question in the context of the contemporary Swedish experience and find a small reduction in male labor supply (2.6 to 3.4 hours per week) related to the presence of one or more young children in the household. Lundberg and Rose (2000) find that in U.S. households where the mother continues to work, the father reduces hours worked substantially. Preston (2000) presents an interesting statistical discrimination model in which employers are unable initially to observe long-term career prospects, but once parenthood occurs, true child care responsibilities are observed and both women and men are tracked correctly into high- or low-career orientation paths. In her data, earnings differentials between men and women fall to zero once the share of child care responsibility is included in the analysis.

To sum up, again there is difficulty in considering all explanations simultaneously, using a data set that has good controls for human capital variables (particularly work experience and intermittency measures) and controlling for heterogeneity and endogeneity. In addition, the philosophical question arises of whether children's indirect effects in reducing labor force attachment should be credited to the children *per se*. However, without crediting these indirect effects, the effects of children on female labor market behavior appear to be relatively small.

OTHER FAMILY STRUCTURE EFFECTS

Now that we have considered the two main veins of the research literature on family structure effects, we turn briefly to outlining other topics that are of interest but have received less focus by researchers. A number of persons have been interested in the recent rise in cohabitation, particularly in this country and in Western Europe, particularly in Sweden (Waite and Gallagher 2000). Cohabitation appears to have some of the productivity advantages of married life, such as the possibility of day-to-day specialization. But it lacks the ones that rely on a long-term relationship, as such couples are not willing to specialize more completely, given the uncertainty inherent in a nonformal relationship.

Another phenomenon of some interest is the increased number and proportion of dual-earner couples, mainly in the United States, in which the wife earns more than the husband (Winkler 1998). While this is an outcomes measure, it also has implications for how bargaining in the home is affected, an area of increased research in general by theoreticians. Another phenomenon of interest concurrent with the increase in dual-earner couples is the apparent rise in correlation between husbands' and wives' earnings. This is in contrast to the earlier argument that high-earner husbands might well pick wives who had relatively high nonmarket production capabilities, a feature that was assumed to be generally negatively correlated with high market production capability (Nakosteen and Zimmer 2001). This has been of particular interest for its implications regarding income inequality between families, although so far changes in wives' earnings do not explain a substantial portion of the rise in family income inequality that has occurred since the 1980s (Cancian and Reed 1999).

Another topic that has been barely studied yet in a systematic empirical way is the implications of the rising number of elderly and how they may be cared for in both resident and nonresident settings by their close relatives. A related topic is how families deal with disabled members of any age. It is known that a majority of caregivers for both household members and persons outside the household are women (Schmittroth 1991, Tables 111, 113). It appears that the existence of a dependent elder in a family household is negatively correlated with earnings of adults in their immediate family (Tilly and Albelda 1994); linkages with nonresident dependent elders, where effects may operate through the need to provide both time and money toward their care, have yet to be clearly measured in terms of their effects on labor market outcomes for caregivers. For instance, one study finds no evidence of reduced employment among married women caregivers (Wolf and Soldo 1994), while other studies find that caregivers have significantly reduced employment (Ettner 1995; White-Means 1992).

Finally, a number of studies have considered labor market effects related to the situation of one's birth family rather than one's current family. While some studies (Neumark and Korenman 1994) have exploited sibling and parental relationships in an attempt to control for unobservables that are correlated across family members, others have considered directly the effects of family size, birth order, and/or sibling gender mix on one's own outcomes. These effects have in large part been modeled as affecting one's human capital investments, such as educational attainment, prior to entering the labor market. Regarding family size, Kessler (1991) finds no effect on wages but finds some relation to labor supply for women—women from small families work less when young, more when older. Regarding birth order effects, Behrman and Taubman (1986) find favorable labor market outcomes for first-born children, Kessler finds no effect on wages of birth order, and Oettinger (2000) finds that older sibling educational achievement positively affects younger sibling educational achievement. Regarding sibling gender mix, Butcher and Case (1994) find that women raised only with brothers received more education than women raised with any sisters. In contrast, Kaestner (1997) finds no such effect among whites, and finds that among blacks, sisters are positively related to educational attainment, while Hauser and Kuo (1998) find no effect of sibling gender composition on educational attainment.

While the aforementioned studies all use contemporary U.S. data, these topics have also been considered using historical data (Sassler 1995) and data from developing countries—indeed, birth family structure effects appear to be of increasing interest now that more data are available from these countries that allow for empirical research. In the developing country context, interest has centered on health indicators as well as educational indicators, and effects appear larger. For example, Garg and Morduch (1998), using Ghanaian data, find that children with sisters but no brothers score 25 to 40 percent better on measured health indicators than if they have only brothers. A final topic, continuing linkages to one's birth family (without necessarily implying any type of direct income or hours transfers), has barely been considered, although Neumark and Postlewaite (1998) find that relative income comparisons to one's sisters and sisters-in-law are significant in explaining the increase in female labor supply.

POLICY-RELEVANT CONCLUSIONS

In conclusion, let us briefly consider two questions. Does family structure matter enough for labor market outcomes that we should do anything about it? If so, what should we do? From my preceding discussion, it is clear that I think it is far from obvious that these effects are large enough to cause concern. But even if they were large, the issue of whether there is anything amiss here is not obvious.

If the premia and penalties we observe were clearly the result of prejudicial discrimination, as opposed to being based on productivity differences, compensating differentials, or marriage market matching, then we would want to eradicate it. This is the argument given for making sex and race discrimination illegal, and indeed, we also make questions regarding one's family status illegal for employers to ask. However, unlike sex and race discrimination, because family status is a choice variable and is changeable, it is less obvious that anything should be done. The usual argument that discrimination is distortionary would hold, but it is apparently discrimination against women as a whole that is problematic, not necessarily against women who are married mothers. Policy proposals that reduce discrimination against women in general would have the effect of raising the return to investments in their human capital, regardless of either their expectations or outcomes regarding marriage and child rearing.

One conclusion we can draw from positive marriage premiums for both working men and women (and potentially positive premiums achieved by those who specialize in nonmarket production as well) is that marriage is an efficiency-raising device, which might be encouraged therefore on efficiency grounds alone. Indeed, Waite and Gallagher (2000) argues a strong case for taking societal actions to strengthen society's commitment to the institution of marriage, in part on economic grounds, and in part on a number of other grounds, including its apparent causal linkage to better mental, physical, and emotional health.

But most work/family policy initiatives are suggested in order to reduce the negative outcomes associated with child raising, particularly with raising children while unmarried. These include high rates of poverty and near-poverty for female-headed families, whether created through out-of-wedlock birth or divorce. Direct income transfers and attempts to increase the human capital of such families are two such policies. Note that neither of these need be directly associated with the family structure so much as with the low state of human capital investment in these persons to begin with. Another set of policies attempts to reduce the income penalty associated with taking parental leaves from one's career, or stepping down to part-time work. Paid parental leaves and child care subsidies can have measurable effects, both directly by increasing a family's income, and indirectly by increasing labor force attachment. To the extent that these preserve human capital investments and encourage such investments, they may be viewed as desirable. But prices may also be distorted in a way that reduces the value of nonmarket labor, including child care performed in the household. A clearer case would need to be made, either on the grounds of offsetting current distortions overvaluing such labor, or on the grounds that work/family policies internalize positive externalities of family structure, in order to justify them.

Finally, dependent care assistance, whether for children, the elderly, or the disabled, which could be paid directly to either the dependent or to the caregiver, would reduce the income strain associated with these situations. The latter two, particularly to the degree that elderly persons have high disability rates, appear to be a reasonable form of insurance in cases where various problems causing incomplete insurance markets have made it difficult for individuals and families to self-insure. The former is less defensible on insurance grounds if one believes that child raising is a freely chosen option, with many of its benefits accruing to the family itself.

However, insuring against negative outcomes caused by the circumstances of one's birth is a reasonable policy to consider. Assistance targeted to those children who receive negative outcomes (such as low educational attainment) because of parental investment decisions (and potentially lack of investment funds due to capital market constraints) would be defensible as a social insurance program against being born in a family situation where you do not receive as good an outcome as those in other, more fortunate family situations. For instance, for a society in which there is systematic underinvestment in girls by their families, societal leaders could make the decision to offset this underinvestment. This is clearly an area that needs consideration in a number of developing countries.

The issue therefore appears to come down to choice: To what degree is the choice of family situation made freely? What sorts of constraints (in the usual economist terms of relative prices and endowments) operate on that choice? In all societies, one does not choose what family to be born into, and we have strong equity grounds for minimizing the differences caused by birth family circumstance. In some societies, arguably including our own, one does choose what family to create, and the equity grounds for minimizing differences in labor market outcomes related to that choice are therefore much less clear.

In conclusion, while the robustness—and policy relevance—of the findings presented in this chapter is ambiguous, I have found the effects of family structure on labor outcomes an intriguing area to explore. Much remains to be done on this topic, and I look forward to reading, as well as doing my own research, in this area for years to come.

References

Behrman, Jere R., and Paul Taubman. 1986. "Birth Order, Schooling, and Earnings." *Journal of Labor Economics* 4(3, part 2): S121–S145.

Blackaby, D.H., P.S. Carlin, and P.D. Murphy. 1998. "What a Difference a Wife Makes: The Effect of Women's Hours of Work on Husbands' Hourly Earnings." *Bulletin of Economic Research* 50(1): 1–18.

Blackburn, McKinley, and Sanders Korenman. 1994. "The Declining Marital-Status Earnings Differential." *Journal of Population Economics* 7(3): 247–270.

Butcher, Kristin F., and Anne Case. 1994. "The Effect of Sibling Sex Composition on Women's Education and Earnings." *Quarterly Journal of Economics* 109(3): 531–563.

Cancian, Maria, and Deborah Reed. 1999. "The Impact of Wives' Earnings on Income Inequality: Issues and Estimates." *Demography* 36(2): 173–184.

Cappelli, Peter, Jill Constantine, and Clint Chadwick. 2000. "It Pays to Value Family: Work and Family Tradeoffs Reconsidered." *Industrial Relations* 39(2): 175–198.

Carlin, Paul S., and Lennart Flood. 1997. "Do Children Affect the Labor Supply of Swedish Men? Time Diary vs. Survey Data." *Labour Economics* 4(2): 167–183.

Chalmers, Jenny. 1996. "Wages of Married Men and Hours Worked in the Labour Market by Their Wives: Is There a Linkage?" Working Paper, Australian National University, Canberra, New South Wales.

Chun, Hyunbae, and Injae Lee. 2001. "Why Do Married Men Earn More: Productivity or Marriage Selection?" *Economic Inquiry* 39(2): 307–319.

Cohen, Yinon, and Yitchak Haberfeld. 1991. "Why Do Married Men Earn More than Unmarried Men?" *Social Science Research* 20(1): 29–44.

Cornwell, Christopher, and Peter Rupert. 1995. "Marriage and Earnings." *Federal Reserve Bank of Cleveland Economic Review* 31(4): 10–20.

Ettner, Susan L. 1995. "The Impact of 'Parent Care' on Female Labor Supply Decisions." *Demography* 32(1): 63–80.

Garg, Ashish, and Jonathan Morduch. 1998. "Sibling Rivalry and the Gender Gap: Evidence from Child Health Outcomes in Ghana." *Journal of Population Economics* 11(4): 471–493.

Gray, Jeffrey S. 1997. "The Fall in Men's Return to Marriage: Declining Productivity Effects or Changing Selection?" *Journal of Human Resources* 32(3): 481–504.

Gray, Jeffrey S., and Michel J. Vanderhart. 2000. "On the Determination of Wages: Does Marriage Matter?" In *The Ties That Bind: Perspectives on Marriage and Cohabitation*, Linda J. Waite, ed. New York, New York: Aldine de Gruyter, pp. 356–367.

Harkness, Susan, and Jane Waldfogel. 1999. "The Family Gap in Pay: Evidence from Seven Industrialised Countries." Centre for Analysis of Social Exclusion Discussion Paper CASE/30, London School of Economics, London, United Kingdom.

Hauser, Robert M., and Hsiang-Hui Daphne Kuo. 1998. "Does the Gender Composition of Sibships Affect Women's Educational Attainment?" *Journal of Human Resources* 33(3): 644–657.

Hersch, Joni. 1991a. "The Impact of Nonmarket Work on Market Wages." *American Economic Review* 81(2): 157–160.

———. 1991b. "Male-Female Differences in Hourly Wages: The Role of Human Capital, Working Conditions, and Housework." *Industrial & Labor Relations Review* 44(4): 746–759.

Hersch, Joni, and Leslie S. Stratton. 1997. "Housework, Fixed Effects, and Wages of Married Workers." *Journal of Human Resources* 32(2): 285–307.

———. 2000. "Household Specialization and the Male Marriage Wage Premium." *Industrial and Labor Relations Review* 54(1): 78–94.

———. 2002. "Housework and Wages." *Journal of Human Resources* 37(1): 217–229.

Hill, Martha S. 1979. "The Wage Effects of Marital Status and Children." *Journal of Human Resources* 14(4): 579–594.

Hotchkiss, Julie L., and Robert E. Moore. 1999. "On the Evidence of a Working Spouse Penalty in the Managerial Labor Market." *Industrial & Labor Relations Review* 52(3): 410–423.

Jacobsen, Joyce P., and Laurence M. Levin. 1995. "Effects of Intermittent Labor Force Attachment on Women's Earnings." *Monthly Labor Review* 118(9): 14–19.

Jacobsen, Joyce P., James Wishart Pearce III, and Joshua L. Rosenbloom. 1999. "The Effects of Child-Bearing on Married Women's Labor Supply and Earnings: Using Twin Births as a Natural Experiment." *Journal of Human Resources* 34(3): 449–474.

Jacobsen, Joyce P., and Wendy L. Rayack. 1996. "Do Men Whose Wives Work Really Earn Less?" *American Economic Review* 86(2): 268–273.

Joshi, Heather, Susan Macran, and Shirley Dex. 1996. "Employment after Childbearing and Women's Subsequent Labour Force Participation: Evidence from the British 1958 Birth Cohort." *Journal of Population Economics* 9(3): 325–348.

Joshi, Heather, Susan Macran, Shirley Dex, Pierella Paci, and Jane Waldfogel. 1999. "The Wages of Motherhood: Better or Worse?" *Cambridge Journal of Economics* 23(5): 543–564.

Kaestner, Robert. 1997. "Are Brothers Really Better? Sibling Sex Composition and Educational Achievement Revisited." *Journal of Human Resources* 32(2): 250–284.

Kessler, Daniel. 1991. "Birth Order, Family Size, and Achievement: Family Structure and Wage Determination." *Journal of Labor Economics* 9(4): 413–426.

Korenman, Sanders, and David Neumark. 1991. "Does Marriage Really Make Men More Productive?" *Journal of Human Resources* 26(2): 282–307.

————. 1992. "Marriage, Motherhood, and Wages." *Journal of Human Resources* 27(2): 233–255.

Loh, Eng Seng. 1996. "Productivity Differences and the Marriage Wage Premium for White Males." *Journal of Human Resources* 31(3): 566–589.

Lundberg, Shelly, and Elaina Rose. 2000. "Parenthood and the Earnings of Married Men and Women." *Labour Economics* 7(6): 689–710.

Nakosteen, Robert A., and Michael A. Zimmer. 1987. "Marital Status and Earnings of Young Men: A Model with Endogenous Selection." *Journal of Human Resources* 22(2): 248–268.

————. 1997. "Men, Money, and Marriage: Are High Earners More Prone Than Low Earners to Marry?" *Social Science Quarterly* 78(1): 66–82.

————. 2001. "Spouse Selection and Earnings: Evidence of Marital Sorting." *Economic Inquiry* 39(2): 201–213.

Netz, Janet S., and Jon D. Haveman. 1999. "All in the Family: Family, Income, and Labor Force Attachment." *Feminist Economics* 5(3): 85–106.

Neumark, David, and Sanders Korenman. 1994. "Sources of Bias in Women's Wage Equations: Results Using Sibling Data." *Journal of Human Resources* 29(2): 379–405.

Neumark, David, and Andrew Postlewaite. 1998. "Relative Income Concerns and the Rise in Married Women's Employment." *Journal of Public Economics* 70(1): 157–183.

Oettinger, Gerald S. 2000. "Sibling Similarity in High School Graduation Outcomes: Causal Interdependency or Unobserved Heterogeneity?" *Southern Economic Journal* 66(3): 631–648.

Pfeffer, Jeffrey, and Jerry Ross. 1982. "The Effects of Marriage and a Working Wife on Occupational and Wage Attainment." *Administrative Science Quarterly* 27(1): 66–80.

Preston, Anne E. 2000. "Sex, Kids, and Commitment to the Workplace: Employers, Employees and the Mommy Track." Working Paper, Haverford College, Haverford, Pennsylvania.

Reed, W. Robert, and Kathleen Harford. 1989. "The Marriage Premium and Compensating Wage Differentials." *Journal of Population Economics* 2(4): 237–265.

Rose, David C., and Anne E. Winkler. 2000. "Career Hierarchy in Dual-Earner Families." In *Research in Labor Economics* 19, Solomon Polachek, ed. Greenwich, Connecticut: JAI Press, pp. 147–172.

Rosenzweig, Mark R., and Kenneth I. Wolpin. 2000. "Natural 'Natural Experiments' in Economics." *Journal of Economic Literature* 38(4): 827–874.

Sassler, Sharon. 1995. "Trade-Offs in the Family: Sibling Effects on Daughters' Activities in 1910." *Demography* 32(4): 557–575.

Stratton, Leslie S. 2001. "Why Does More Housework Lower Women's Wages? Testing Hypotheses Involving Job Effort and Hours Flexibility." *Social Science Quarterly* 82(1): 67–76.

Schmittroth, Linda. 1991. *Statistical Record of Women Worldwide.* Detroit, Michigan: Gale Research.

Tilly, Chris, and Randy Albelda. 1994. "Family Structure and Family Earnings: The Determinants of Earnings Differences among Family Types." *Industrial Relations* 33(2): 151–167.

U.S. Department of Commerce, Bureau of the Census. 1999. Current Population Survey: Annual Demographic File, 1999 [Computer file]. Washington, D.C.: U.S. Department of Commerce, Bureau of the Census.

————. 2000. *Statistical Abstract of the United States.* Washington, D.C.: U.S. Department of Commerce, Bureau of the Census.

U.S. Department of Labor, Bureau of Labor Statistics. 1995. "Glossary of Subject Concepts." http://www.bls.census.gov/cps/ads/1995/sglosary.htm.

Waite, Linda J., and Maggie Gallagher. 2000. *The Case for Marriage: Why Married People Are Happier, Healthier, and Better Off Financially.* New York: Doubleday.

Waldfogel, Jane. 1998. "Understanding the 'Family Gap' in Pay for Women with Children." *Journal of Economic Perspectives.*12(1): 137–156.

White-Means, Shelley I. 1992. "Allocation of Labor to Informal Home Health Production: Health Care for Frail Elderly, if Time Permits." *Journal of Consumer Affairs* 26(1): 69–89.

Winkler, Anne E. 1998. "Earnings of Husbands and Wives in Dual-Earner Families." *Monthly Labor Review* 121(4): 42–48.

Wolf, Douglas A. and Beth J. Soldo. 1994. "Married Women's Allocation of Time to Employment and Care of Elderly Parents." *Journal of Human Resources* 29(4): 1259–1276.

6
Working for All Families? Family Leave Policies in the United States

Katherin Ross Phillips
The Urban Institute

Over the past 20 years, two demographic trends in the United States have captured the attention of social scientists and policymakers. First, the percentage of mothers with young children who are in the workforce has increased. Today most children with married parents see both their mother and father go to work each week, and single parents are more likely to work full time than either part time or not at all (Ross Phillips 2002). As parents become increasingly attached to the labor market, pressures build within employers and across governments to develop working environments that facilitate the combination of caregiving and market work responsibilities. Adding to these pressures is the second major demographic trend of the late twentieth century: the aging of the population. As they age, workers' need for leave from work to tend to their own health or to care for their parents or spouses intensifies.

In 1993, the United States passed legislation aimed at easing the tension many employees feel as they face the challenge of trying to care for themselves and their families while maintaining an attachment to the workforce. The Family and Medical Leave Act (FMLA) provides job-protected leave to eligible workers for a variety of caregiving and medical reasons. Throughout the 1990s state governments and private employers also experimented with different leave policies.

Policies that allow workers time to take care of their own and their families' health needs can improve employment security in the short-term and, as a result, help raise family earnings and income in the long-term. Explicit in the FMLA is a goal to promote economic security for all families (U.S. Department of Labor 1993). The ability of family policies, both public and private, to improve economic security depends both on benefit generosity and the number of workers who have access to the benefits. If access to family leave is negatively related to income status, then the economic security derived from family leave may not reach low-income working caregivers. For example, poor mothers who leave the welfare system for employment may find they are not protected by the FMLA.

Just three years after passing the FMLA, the United States enacted the Personal Responsibility and Work Opportunities Reconciliation Act of 1996 (PRWORA). Commonly referred to as "welfare reform," a goal of the legislation is to convert welfare into a transitional, work-focused assistance program. The law requires most participants to work after two years of benefit receipt and imposes a five-year lifetime limit on a family's receipt of the federal portion of welfare benefits. As a result, the PRWORA will move mothers who previously relied on public support into the workforce. Given that federal policy is directing some welfare recipients into employment, it seems reasonable to ask if federally guaranteed employment supports, such as the FMLA, are available to these mothers.

This chapter examines whether leave provided under the FMLA, as well as through private employers and state policies, works for all families in the United States. After reviewing the forms of leave that workers might use to address their family and medical needs, the chapter looks at whether access to these benefits is related to family income or occupations status. Research suggests that in the years directly after leaving welfare for work, most mothers will be employed in blue-collar or service occupations and will live in families with incomes less than twice the poverty line. The analysis highlights these occupation and income groups. The chapter concludes with some policy recommendations aimed at improving access to family leave benefits among low-income workers.

PUBLIC AND PRIVATE FAMILY LEAVE POLICIES

The Family and Medical Leave Act of 1993

The FMLA was the first major piece of legislation signed into law by President Clinton. The act provides eligible employees with up to 12 unpaid work weeks of job-protected leave during any 12-month period for the birth or adoption of a child, the foster care of a child, to care for a seriously ill child, spouse, or parent, or for an employee's own serious illness.

Leave mandated by the FMLA is job-protected but unpaid. After an FMLA leave the employer must allow a leave-taker to return either to the same position held before the leave or to a position with equivalent pay, benefits, terms of employment, and seniority. An employer may deny reinstatement to an employee who is among the highest paid 10 percent of the employer's workforce if reinstatement would cause "substantial and grievous economic injury" to the business. Furthermore, if the employee would have been laid off, terminated, or downgraded had she not taken leave, her job will not be protected during her leave.

The FMLA does not require remuneration during the leave period. An employer, however, may require its employees to use accrued vacation and/or sick leave as a portion of FMLA leave. An employee can use paid vacation or annual leave for a portion of FMLA leave and will usually be permitted to use paid, accrued sick leave as well. The total amount of FMLA leave, however, cannot exceed 12 weeks within a 12-month period. For example, if an employee substitutes two paid vacation weeks for FMLA leave, then she is only entitled to 10 unpaid weeks.

The use of FMLA leave cannot result in the loss of any employment benefit earned prior to the leave, although benefits need not accrue during the leave. Under the FMLA, an employer must maintain health insurance coverage during the leave period in the same manner as if the employee had continued employment. If the employee fails to return to work after the specified leave period an employer can stop paying for health insurance and recover premiums paid to maintain the health insurance during the leave period. If the employee cannot return to work due to a continued health condition or a reason beyond the employee's control, however, the employer cannot recover health insurance premiums paid during the leave period.

Family and medical leave is available to an employee who 1) has at least 12 months of tenure with the employer from whom she will take leave; 2) has worked at least 1,250 hours during the 12 months preceding the leave period for the employer; and 3) works for an employer who employs at least 50 people within a 75-mile radius of the employee's worksite. The FMLA applies to private establishments, federal, state, and local governments, and Congress. The FMLA does not replace any state legislation that was more generous than the FMLA's provisions.

According to a recent Department of Labor survey, of the six possible reasons for taking family leave, a worker's own serious health condition is the most common (Cantor et al. 2001).[1] Among workers who took family leave over an 18-month period ending last year, the majority (52 percent) of the workers took leave for their own serious illnesses. Less than one in five workers took parental leave (19 percent), and 8 percent took leave for maternity disability.[2] Similar percentages of workers took leave to care for a seriously ill parent (13 percent) or child (12 percent). Only 6 percent of workers used leave to care for an ill spouse.

State Family Leave Policies

Some state laws provide family leave that is more expansive than the FMLA. For example, a number of states allow longer maternity and parental leave periods, some states mandate that small employers also provide maternity leave, and a few states allow parents some time away from market work to participate in their children's education. State Temporary Disability Insurance (TDI) programs in California, Hawaii, New Jersey, New York, and Rhode Island provide partial wage replacement during maternity disability leaves. Typically, TDI leaves are not job-protected, and eligibility criteria for TDI programs can limit their reach. Minnesota's At-Home Infant Child Care program allows some low-income working families to collect child care subsidies while parents stay at home to care for their own infants under one year of age. Participation in the program and funding have been quite limited.

Over the past three years, there has been a lot of activity at the state level to pass a variety of family leave laws. Most states have focused on developing ways to provide some remuneration during FMLA leaves. To date, however, no state has enacted comprehensive family leave legislation.[3] Some of the recent state proposals are discussed in the policy options section at the end of this chapter.

Employer Policies

Employer policies have often provided some workers with leave that they could take for a subset of family leave purposes. Employers might offer paid sick leave that an employee can use for her own illness and, in some cases, to care for her sick child; short-term disability leave that can often be used for maternity leave purposes; paid vacations that can generally be used for any purpose provided the employee gives sufficient notice; and paid personal leave that typically allows workers to take time off for reasons not covered by other leave policies. Increasingly, employers have begun to offer some employees packages of "unrestricted leave." Under this benefit, employees have access to a specified number of paid days of leave that they can use for any reason.

In place of formal leave policies, firms may also permit leaves of absence for some family leave purposes on a case-by-case basis. Although data on informal family leave policies are not consistently collected, maternity leave coverage estimates increase when they include the informal mechanisms for maternity leave provision. While 36 percent of firms surveyed in a study during the mid 1980s had formal policies, an additional 50 percent had informal policies (Raabe and Gessner 1988).

Informal policies and the use of sick leave, vacation time, and personal leave to provide family leave may restrict access to leave. Sick leave and vacation time accrue slowly and are often capped at a relatively small number of weeks. Caregivers who have short job tenures may not be able to accrue a sufficient number of weeks of leave for family leave purposes—especially for childbearing and parental leaves. Using accrued vacation and sick leave for family leave also reduces the opportunities for additional time off in a year during which a caregiver experiences the stresses of childbirth, new parenthood, or illness. Workers who use accrued vacation and sick leave for family leaves are not guaranteed to have their jobs available when they return to market work unless the leaves are covered under the FMLA.

Both public and private family leave policies can help covered and eligible workers combine their family and work responsibilities. The following sections examine who is covered and who is eligible for family leave. To gauge whether low-income workers, particularly recent welfare-leavers, have equal access to family leave benefits, the analyses focuses on the income status and occupations of workers who have and who do not have access to family leave benefits.

ACCESS TO FAMILY LEAVE: COVERAGE

Family and Medical Leave Act

Family and medical leave is only available to persons who work for relatively large firms. At the end of the twentieth century, about 58 percent of workers in private establishments were covered under the FMLA (Cantor et al. 2001). Research suggests that women who successfully transition from welfare to market work will remain low income in the short term. Table 1 compares the firm sizes of workers

Table 1 Percent of Workers in Different Firm Sizes, by Income Status, 1999

	Family income less than twice the poverty line	Family income above twice the poverty line
Number of employees at worksite		
Less than 25	43.3	30.4
25–49	13.0	11.3
50–100	12.6	11.8
More than 100	31.1	46.5

SOURCE: Author's calculations of the 1999 National Survey of America's Families.

with family incomes less than twice the poverty line to the firm sizes of high-income workers.[4] More than 56 percent of low-income workers are employed at worksites with fewer than 50 employees compared to less than 42 percent of higher income workers. The data in Table 1 suggest that the majority of low-income workers are probably not covered by the FMLA.[5]

State Policies

A primary way state policies provide more generous leaves than the FMLA is through expanded coverage. The District of Columbia, Oregon, and Vermont all provide some form of family leave to employees of firms that are smaller than firms covered by the FMLA. Laws in California, Connecticut, Hawaii, Iowa, Louisiana, Maine, Massachusetts, Minnesota, Montana, and New Hampshire mandate that smaller employers than are covered under the FMLA provide maternity benefits to working women in their states. States that set very low firm-size thresholds for leave coverage (e.g., below 10 employees) may increase the share of low-income workers that are covered by public family leave policies.

Private Establishment Policies

Each year the Bureau of Labor Statistics (BLS) surveys private establishments to gather information about the types of benefits they provide to their workers. In even years the BLS surveys small establishments, firms with fewer than 100 employees; in odd years, the BLS surveys medium and large establishments, firms with at least 100 employees. Tables 2 and 3 summarize some of the data collected in these surveys for full-time employees in 1996 and 1997. Patterns are similar for part-time employees, but coverage rates are substantially smaller.

The differential impact of the FMLA by firm size is noticeable in the first two rows of Table 2. Some proportion of the small firms in Table 2 are covered by the FMLA either because they employ 50 to 100 employees or because they have a number of worksites within a small geographical area. However, fewer than half of workers in small establishments have access to unpaid family leave, compared to 93 percent of workers in large firms. Blue-collar and service workers are the

Table 2 Full-Time Employees Covered by Various Leave Policies, by Occupation

		Types of employees		
	All	Professional, technical, and related	Clerical and sales	Blue-collar and service
Unpaid family leave				
Large firms[a]	93	95	96	91
Small firms[b]	48	53	52	43
Paid family leave				
Large firms	2	3	3	1
Small firms	2	3	3	1
Paid sick leave				
Large firms	56	73	73	38
Small firms	50	66	64	35
Short-term disability				
Large firms	55	54	52	58
Small firms	29	32	33	25
Paid vacations				
Large firms	95	96	97	94
Small firms	86	90	95	79
Paid personal leave				
Large firms	20	23	33	13
Small firms	14	21	18	8

[a] Large firms are establishments with at least 100 employees. The Bureau of Labor Statistics refers to these as medium and large establishments. Data for large firms are from 1997.

[b] Small firms are establishments with fewer than 100 employees. Data for small firms are from 1996.

SOURCE: U.S. Bureau of Labor Statistics (1999a,b).

least likely to have unpaid family leave. Only 2 percent of workers in either small or large firms receive paid family leave. Across all other leave types, employees in larger firms are more likely to have access to leave than employees in small establishments and blue-collar and service employees are the least likely occupation group to have access to all forms of leave.

Average length of leave available for covered employees varies by firm size and occupation (Table 3). In general, full-time employees in small private firms are covered under leave policies that are shorter in duration than the policies found in larger private firms. Within large firms, blue-collar and service employees are covered by leave policies that have shorter average durations than policies that apply to the other occupation groups. For example, after one year of service, professional/technical employees in private establishments with more than 100 employees are entitled to an average of 13.3 paid sick days while blue-collar and service employees in large, private establishments are entitled to an average of 9.9 days of sick leave. Blue-collar and service workers are the least likely to be allowed to carry over their sick leave from year to year and are the most likely to end up in a "use or lose" situation at the end of the plan year (U.S. Bureau of Labor Statistics 1999a,b).

Within private establishments, blue-collar and service workers are less likely to have access to leave that may be used for family leave purposes. Some firms allow workers to use their sick leave to care for a sick child. The percentage of workers who can use sick leave to care for a sick child varies by the size of the firm and occupation and ranges from a low of 43 percent for blue-collar and service workers in large firms to a high of 63 percent of professional and technical workers in small establishments (U.S. Bureau of Labor Statistics 1999a,b).

A few patterns emerge from the BLS data. Establishments that employ fewer than 100 people are typically less likely to provide leave to their workers than larger employers. Among the small firms that do provide leave, average available leave length is generally shorter. Workers in blue-collar and service occupations have less access to private family leave policies than workers in other occupations. Low-income workers tend to work for smaller firms than higher-income workers (see Table 1). Using data from the National Survey of America's Families (NSAF), Table 4 demonstrates that low-income and

Table 3 Average Length of Leave Available For Covered Full-Time Employees, by Occupation

		Types of employees		
	All	Professional, technical, and related	Clerical and sales	Blue-collar and service
Unpaid family leave (weeks)				
Large firms[a]	14.0	14.8	14.3	13.4
Small firms[b]	12.5	12.4	12.6	12.4
Paid family leave (weeks)				
Large firms	NA	NA	NA	NA
Small firms	NA	NA	NA	NA
Paid sick leave (days)[c,d,e]				
Large firms	11.2	13.3	10.1	9.9
Small firms	8.0	7.6	7.6	8.8
Short-term disability (weeks)[f]				
Large firms	25	25	24	26
Small firms	25	24	24	26
Paid vacations (days)[c]				
Large firms	9.6	12.4	9.9	7.9
Small firms	8.1	10.0	8.6	6.8
Paid personal leave (days)				
Large firms	3.5	3.5	3.3	3.6
Small firms	3.0	3.1	2.9	2.9

NOTE: NA = not available.

[a] Large firms are establishments with at least 100 employees. The U.S. Bureau of Labor Statistics refers to these as medium and large establishments. Data for large firms are from 1997.

[b] Small firms are establishments with fewer than 100 employees. Data for small firms are from 1996.

[c] Average number of days available after one year of service for covered employees.

[d] Paid sick leave durations are calculated only for covered employees whose paid sick leave policy provides for a specific number of days. Nine percent of employees in large firms and 13 percent of employees in small firms are covered under sick leave policies that provide leave on an "as needed" or other basis. Most of these employees work in professional/technical occupations.

[e] Data for sick leave durations are aggregated by white-collar and blue-collar in U.S. Bureau of Labor Statistics (1999a).

[f] Short-term disability durations are calculated only for covered employees whose short-term disability policy is for a fixed duration. Three percent of employees in small businesses and 5 percent of employees in large firms are covered under policies that have a variable duration. Most of these employees work in the clerical or sales occupations.

SOURCE: U.S. Bureau of Labor Statistics (1999a,b).

Table 4 Percent of Employees in Different Occupations, by Income Status, 1999

	Family income less than twice the poverty line	Family income above twice the poverty line
Occupation		
Professional/technical	14.1	38.6
Clerical and sales	23.4	25.1
Blue-collar and service	62.5	36.3

SOURCE: Author's calculations of the 1999 National Survey of America's Families.

poor workers are more likely to work in blue-collar and service occupations. Nearly 63 percent of low-income workers are employed in blue-collar and service occupations, compared to just over 36 percent of higher-income workers.

Summary: Family Leave Coverage

Coverage of both public and private leave policies tends to disproportionately exclude low-income workers and workers in blue-collar and service occupations. Low-income workers are more likely to live in families with children than higher-income workers (Acs et al. 2000). As a result they may have a greater need for family leave than higher-income workers. Assuming they look more like low-income than higher-income workers, former welfare participants who move into the workforce may not be covered by either private or public family leave policies that could facilitate their transition from focusing on caregiving toward combining caregiving with market work.

ACCESS TO FAMILY LEAVE: ELIGIBILITY

Family and Medical Leave Act

Although nearly 58 percent of all U.S. workers in private establishments are covered under the FMLA, not all of these workers meet the act's eligibility criteria. Only workers who have worked for their employers for at least 12 months and for at least 1,250 hours over the past year are eligible to take FMLA leave. Approximately 81 percent of all workers who report that they work at a worksite that meets the FMLA coverage restrictions also report that they meet the job tenure and hours requirements of the legislation (Cantor et al. 2001). Assuming that the estimated share of workers who meet the eligibility requirements applies to the subset of workers employed at private establishments, roughly 47 percent of workers in private industry are both covered and eligible for FMLA leave.[6]

Low-income workers are much less likely to meet the eligibility requirements than workers living in higher-income families. Only 54 percent of workers with annual family incomes less than $20,000, who are covered under the FMLA, meet the eligibility criteria. In contrast, nearly 89 percent of workers with annual family incomes above $50,000, who are covered under the FMLA, meet the eligibility criteria (author's calculations from data presented in Cantor et al. 2001).

State Policies

Eligibility for state family leaves differs from state to state. Typically, however, employees must work full time to be eligible. Many state laws also include a job tenure requirement. Both hours and job tenure requirements tend to make more low-income workers ineligible for benefits than higher-income workers. Job tenure requirements will prevent recent welfare-leavers from accessing benefits.

Private Establishment Policies

Although no comparable data exist on employee eligibility for leave benefits provided through private employer policies in the late 1990s, the BLS does collect information about the length of service required before workers are eligible for vacation leave and paid sick leave. In firms with more than 100 employees, 91 percent of full-time blue-collar and service workers must meet a service requirement, generally one year on the job, before they are eligible to take vacation leave (U.S. Bureau of Labor Statistics 1999b). In contrast, only 78 percent of full-time professional and technical employees in large firms are required to meet a service requirement before they are eligible to take vacation leave. The service requirement for professional and technical occupations is, on average, only six months (U.S. Bureau of Labor Statistics 1999b). A majority of all workers in large firms must work at least three months before they are eligible to take sick leave. The share of blue-collar and service workers in large firms who must meet a tenure requirement before being eligible for sick leave is 73 percent; only 54 percent of professional and technical workers in large firms must meet a tenure requirement.

The data presented from the BLS surveys so far is for full-time employees. The BLS allows survey respondents to define full time. For the majority of workers full time is equal to 30 or more hours per week. Part-time workers are much less likely to have access to private leave policies than full-time workers. For example, only 15 percent of part-time blue-collar and service workers in large firms are covered under a paid sick leave policy. In Table 2 the comparable share among full-time workers is 35 percent.

Summary: Family Leave Eligibility

As was the case with coverage, low-income workers and workers in blue-collar and service occupations are less likely to be eligible for family leave benefits. The service requirements for both private leave policies and the FMLA restrict access to family leave benefits to workers who have some job tenure. As a result, caregivers who are transitioning off of welfare and other new entrants into the workforce will not have family leave protections at their new jobs, even if they work full time.

Access to Family Leave: Take-up

Among workers who have access to some leave from work, taking family leave may be impracticable. For workers who are not covered under the FMLA, their private employer's leave policies may not provide job protection. While the caregiver is out on family leave, her job may be eliminated or given to another employee. Many workers fear that taking leave from work for family leave purposes, especially for caregiving reasons, will have a negative effect on how they are viewed by their supervisors. Research on workplace culture and parental leave suggests that these fears are reasonable (Fried 1998).

Leave guaranteed under the FMLA is unpaid. Low-income workers and primary earners in higher-income families may not be able to forego earnings in order to take family leave. In the Department of Labor's Survey of Employees, the most commonly reported reason for not taking a needed family leave is the inability to afford leave. Seventy-eight percent of leave-needers felt they could not afford to take family leave, and 88 percent of leave-needers said they would have taken leave if they could have received some or additional pay during the leave (Cantor et al. 2001).

Among workers who did take leave, more than one-third received no pay during their longest leave. Receipt of pay during family leave is positively related to income status. Nearly three-quarters of workers with annual incomes less than $20,000 reported receiving no pay during their longest leave. This large percentage does not include low-income workers who were deterred from taking leave because they could not afford it. Among leave-takers who do not receive pay during their leave, nearly 9 percent report using public assistance to replace some of their lost income (Cantor et al. 2001).

POLICIES TO IMPROVE ACCESS TO FAMILY LEAVE

Public policy can address many of the gaps in access to family leave. Given the unequal distribution of family leave access across income strata and occupations, a case for public policy intervention on the grounds of equity could be made. Furthermore, in light of the rhetoric of responsibility and opportunity espoused in the PRWORA, it seems appropriate to provide caregivers transitioning into the workforce an equal opportunity to fulfill both their caregiving and their market work responsibilities.

Since enactment of the FMLA, there have been a number of proposals at the national and state levels to make family leave accessible. Some of these proposals, along with a few novel ideas, are summarized below. In general family leave can be improved to meet the needs of all working families in four broad ways: 1) expand coverage; 2) expand eligibility; 3) expand reasons for leave-taking; and, 4) provide remuneration during the leave.

Expand Coverage

In nearly every session of Congress since 1993, members have introduced a bill that would lower the FMLA establishment size threshold to 25. As stated above, many states provide maternity-leave coverage to women working in small firms. Estimates from the 1999 NSAF suggest that reducing the FMLA threshold to 25 could increase coverage rates by about 12 percentage points distributed fairly evenly across low-income and higher-income workers (see Table 1).[7]

Expand Eligibility

Removing or reducing the job tenure and hours requirements in the FMLA legislation would increase the proportion of covered workers who are eligible for FMLA. Expanding eligibility would be particularly beneficial for low-income workers. Recall that nearly half of covered low-income workers do not meet the FMLA eligibility requirements. New entrants to the workforce, such as recent welfare-leavers, would benefit from a loosening of the job tenure requirement.

Expand Benefits

Proposals at both the state and national levels have attempted to augment the allowable reasons for leave under the FMLA or similar state legislation. In particular, permitting parents to take short periods of time away from market work to attend parent/teacher conferences or to take children to doctors' appointments have been popular proposals. Eight states have successfully enacted leave statutes that allow parents to participate in their children's educational activities. Other proposals for expanding benefits include allowing workers to take leave to care for unrelated persons and for in-laws, expanding the length of leave, and permitting leave for acute, emergency medical conditions. Because low-income workers and welfare-leavers are more likely to have children than higher-income workers, benefits that are targeted toward parents could be particularly beneficial to them.

Provide Remuneration

Proposals to provide some wage replacement during family leaves have received the most public attention. Many states have proposed changes in their Unemployment Insurance (UI) systems or expansions of their Temporary Disability Insurance (TDI) programs. In addition to these two policy options, other public mechanisms for providing wage replacement during family leaves are discussed below.

Unemployment Insurance

In June 2000, the Department of Labor issued regulations allowing states to extend UI benefits to workers on parental leave. With revenue collected through payroll taxes, the UI system provides partial wage replacement for unemployed workers. Each state has its own system for determining both benefit amounts and program eligibility. Typically, workers must meet both job tenure and work hour thresholds before they are eligible for UI benefits. Many state legislatures are debating this option for providing paid leave. As of February 2001, only the Massachusetts legislature had passed "Baby UI" legislation; the governor, however, did not sign the bill.

Using the UI system to provide partial wage replacement during parental leaves would not benefit workers who are eligible for FMLA leave but who do not meet a state's UI eligibility criteria, nor would it provide wage replacement for any other form of family leave. Women and low-income workers are less likely to be eligible for UI benefits than men and higher-income workers (Hobbie, Wittenburg, and Fishman 1999).

Temporary Disability Insurance

Five states and Puerto Rico have TDI programs that provide partial wage replacement to workers with nonwork related, short-term medical disabilities. According to the Pregnancy Discrimination Act of 1978, TDI policies must cover disabilities related to pregnancy and childbirth. TDI plans are funded by employee or employer contributions, or both, and benefit periods range from 26 weeks to 52 weeks. TDI does not guarantee job protection.

The California and New Jersey legislatures have considered expanding their state TDI programs to provide coverage during periods of leave taken for family medical reasons. In 1999, the New York legislature debated allowing workers to collect TDI benefits during any FMLA leave, during leaves for parent/teacher meetings, during bereavement leave, and during leaves to care for household members in medical situations not covered by the FMLA. To date, none of these TDI expansions have become law.

Other Insurance Programs

In Washington State, legislation was recently introduced to develop family leave insurance. The program would be funded through a small payroll tax that employees and employers would split. The insurance fund would provide a flat-rate, weekly stipend for five weeks of family or medical leave.

There is growing concern among some policymakers about the regressive nature of many payroll taxes. Insurance funds could have a progressive funding structure with low-income workers paying in less than higher-income workers. Some employers currently use a sliding-fee scale approach to providing health insurance. This model could be emulated in a family insurance plan.

Family leave insurance funds could also be experience rated.[8] The Department of Labor Employee Survey provides a lot of data about leave-takers that actuaries could use to help develop a model of family and medical leave-taking. With experience rating, public policy could mandate contributions to the family leave insurance fund from all workers. Contributions could be based on an employee's probability of taking leave and the expected amount of wages foregone during that leave. Mandated participation would ensure the largest risk pool and would help avoid problems associated with adverse selection. As a result, family leave insurance funds created through public policy may be preferable to private insurance plans. However, as more caregivers devote an increasing amount of time to the labor force and as the average age of workers increases, a private market for family leave insurance could develop.

Tax Credits and Tax-Preferred Savings

The United States uses its income tax system not only to generate revenue, but also as a means to provide income support to low-income workers and to encourage savings. A refundable tax credit, like the Earned Income Tax Credit, could help ease the financial strain of family leave for low-income families. Unless the tax credit has an advance payment option, the income from the tax credit will probably arrive months after a leave was taken and the income needed. The governor of Massachusetts has proposed a tax credit to employers who provide paid leave to help offset the costs of providing paid leave and to encourage more employers to provide the benefit.

Currently many workers use Flexible Spending Accounts (FSA) to save money for out-of-pocket medical costs and/or child care costs. Contributions to FSAs are made on a pre-tax basis and workers are not required to pay taxes on withdrawals. A tax-preferred savings vehicle modeled after FSAs could help workers save for family leaves. Without either employer contributions or government assistance, however, many low-income workers may not be able to save a sufficient amount to cover wages lost during family leaves.

Welfare Funds

Due to rapidly declining welfare rolls and the relatively fixed block-grant funding stream provided under PRWORA, most states currently have surplus welfare funds. States have considerable discretion in how they spend their surpluses, and they could use a portion of their excess welfare funds to provide paid family leave for low-income workers. Low-income workers and workers in low-wage occupations are the least likely to have access to any paid leave. Targeting publicly funded paid leave at this group of workers could help offset gaps in privately provided leave policies. Using surplus welfare funds to provide welfare-leavers and other low-income workers with affordable access to family leave could help these workers maintain their labor force attachment and promote long-run economic security.

State welfare systems may not always have surpluses. When Congress begins its deliberations over PRWORA reauthorization, the formulas used to determine the size of federal block grants will receive a lot of scrutiny. Funding levels may not continue to exceed the cost of covering core welfare benefits. Furthermore, the rapid decline in welfare participation over the past five years occurred during a strong economy. If the economy weakens, demands on state welfare systems will likely increase. Given the uncertainty of welfare surplus funds, it does not make sense to develop a paid family leave program that relies solely on the existence of a surplus. Nevertheless, welfare surpluses could provide states with a means for testing paid leave programs targeted at low-income populations.

CONCLUSION

Public and private leave policies help many workers combine their caregiving and market work responsibilities. Access to leave benefits, however, is not equal throughout the income distribution and across occupations. Coverage limits, eligibility criteria, and benefit levels combine to limit access to family leave for low-income workers and workers in blue-collar and service occupations. As welfare reform continues to influence the labor market behavior of low-income caregivers, the need for family leave among the population of low-income workers will grow. Public policy can offer these vulnerable workers a better opportunity for a successful transition into the workforce by extending eligibility for family leave and replacing lost earnings during periods of leave.

Notes

Opinions expressed in the paper are those of the author and do not necessarily represent the position of the Urban Institute or its sponsors.

1. This is not necessarily leave taken under the FMLA. Many covered and eligible workers do not know about the FMLA, and very few leave-takers actually ascribe their leave to the FMLA.
2. Respondents could record reasons for more than one family leave. A share of the 8 percent of workers who took maternity leave probably took parental leave as well.
3. See the National Partnership for Women and Families Web site (http://www.nationalpartnership.org) for updated news about state legislative activity.
4. Tables 1 and 4 use data from the National Survey of America's Families (NSAF). The NSAF provides nationally representative estimates for the civilian, noninstitutionalized population under age 65 and their families.
5. The NSAF asks about the number of employees that work at the respondent's worksite. Some of these workers may actually be covered under the FMLA if their employers have additional worksites within a 75-mile radius of the respondent's worksite. In a recent Department of Labor report, more than 91 percent of all FMLA-covered workers were deemed covered because their worksites employed at least 50 workers; less than 9 percent were covered only after considering additional worksites close to the employee's worksite.
6. Data from the 2000 Survey of Employees commissioned by the Department of Labor provides a significantly higher estimate of the percentage of workers covered by the FMLA than data from the 2000 Survey of Establishments, also commissioned by the Department of Labor. The estimated share of covered workers from the Survey of Employees is 77 percent. Although this estimate includes workers in the public as well as the private sector, the estimate is substantially higher than the estimate generated from the Survey of Establishments (58 percent). The estimate derived from the Survey of Employees, if accurate, would suggest a significant increase in the proportion of workers employed in firms that met FMLA coverage criteria from 1995 to 1999. However, BLS data from a similar time period is not suggestive of such an increase. As a result, estimates of the percentage of covered and eligible workers derived from the Department of Labor survey are not reported here. (See Appendix C in Cantor et al. [2001] for a more detailed discussion of the inconsistent estimates.)
7. Most people who work for small businesses work for very small firms—those with fewer than 25 employees. For example, the data in Table 1 suggest that 77 percent of low-income workers employed in worksites with fewer than 50 employees work in firms with fewer than 25 employees (77 percent = 100 x [43.3/(43.3 + 13.0)]). The comparable rate for higher-income workers is 73 percent.
8. The two technical terms in this paragraph—experience rated and adverse selection—are often found in the field of public economics. Insurance companies and

programs use experience ratings to determine how much to charge their clients. Premiums are based on the probability that the insured will experience the activity that the insurance covers. For example, Unemployment Insurance programs determine the tax rate that a firm pays into the program from the firm's history with layoffs.

Adverse selection arises when people who are most likely to receive benefits from insurance are the people who are most likely to purchase insurance. For example, an individual with a chronic health condition that requires treatment may be more likely to purchase health insurance than a healthy person. Very high premium costs can result from adverse selection. Private insurance companies often exclude preexisting conditions from coverage to help dampen the effects of adverse selection.

References

Acs, Gregory, Katherin Ross Phillips, and Daniel McKenzie. 2000. "On the Bottom Rung: A Profile of Americans in Low-Income Working Families." *Assessing the New Federalism,* Policy Brief A-42. The Urban Institute, Washington, D.C., October.

Cantor, David, Jane Waldfogel, Jeffrey Kerwin, Mareena McKinley Wright, Kerry Levin, John Rauch, Tracey Hagerty, and Martha Stapleton Kudela. 2001. *Balancing the Needs of Families and Employers: Family and Medical Leave Surveys.* Report submitted to the U.S. Department of Labor by Westat, Washington, D.C., January.

Fried, Mindy. 1998. *Taking Time: Parental Leave Policy and Corporate Culture.* Philadelphia, Pennsylvania: Temple University Press.

Hobbie, Richard, David Wittenburg, and Michael Fishman. 1999. "Temporary Assistance for Low-Wage Workers: Evolving Relationships among Work, Welfare, and Unemployment Insurance." In *Rethinking Income Support for the Working Poor: Perspectives on Unemployment Insurance, Welfare and Work*, Evelyn Ganzglass and Karen Glass, eds. Washington, D.C.: National Governors' Association Center for Best Practices.

Raabe, P., and J.C. Gessner. 1988. "Employer Family-Supportive Policies: Diverse Variations on the Theme." *Family Relations* 37: 196–202.

Ross Phillips, Katherin E. 2002. "Parent Work and Child Well-Being in Low-Income Families." Assessing the New Federalism Occasional Paper 56, The Urban Institute, Washington, D.C.

U.S. Bureau of Labor Statistics. 1999a. *Employee Benefits in Small Private Establishments, 1996.* Bulletin 2507. Department of Labor, Washington, D.C., April.

————. 1999b. *Employee Benefits in Medium and Large Private Establishments, 1996.* Bulletin 2517. Department of Labor, Washington, D.C., September.

U.S. Department of Labor. 1993. *Family and Medical Leave Act of 1993: Public Law 103-3.* Wage and Hour Division Publication 1418. Employment and Standards Administration., Washington, D.C., May.

Index

The italic letters *f*, *n*, and *t* following a page number indicate that the subject information is within a figure, note, or table, respectively, on that page.

About the Institute

The W.E. Upjohn Institute for Employment Research is a nonprofit research organization devoted to finding and promoting solutions to employment-related problems at the national, state, and local levels. It is an activity of the W.E. Upjohn Unemployment Trustee Corporation, which was established in 1932 to administer a fund set aside by the late Dr. W.E. Upjohn, founder of The Upjohn Company, to seek ways to counteract the loss of employment income during economic downturns.

The Institute is funded largely by income from the W.E. Upjohn Unemployment Trust, supplemented by outside grants, contracts, and sales of publications. Activities of the Institute comprise the following elements: 1) a research program conducted by a resident staff of professional social scientists; 2) a competitive grant program, which expands and complements the internal research program by providing financial support to researchers outside the Institute; 3) a publications program, which provides the major vehicle for disseminating the research of staff and grantees, as well as other selected works in the field; and 4) an Employment Management Services division, which manages most of the publicly funded employment and training programs in the local area.

The broad objectives of the Institute's research, grant, and publication programs are to 1) promote scholarship and experimentation on issues of public and private employment and unemployment policy, and 2) make knowledge and scholarship relevant and useful to policymakers in their pursuit of solutions to employment and unemployment problems.

Current areas of concentration for these programs include causes, consequences, and measures to alleviate unemployment; social insurance and income maintenance programs; compensation; workforce quality; work arrangements; family labor issues; labor-management relations; and regional economic development and local labor markets.